Leading by Story

Rethinking Church Leadership

Vaughan S. Roberts
and
David Sims

scm press

Published in 2017 by SCM Press
Editorial office
3rd Floor, Invicta House,
108–114 Golden Lane,
London EC1Y 0TG, UK

www.scmpress.co.uk

SCM Press is an imprint of Hymns Ancient & Modern Ltd
(a registered charity)

Hymns Ancient & Modern® is a registered trademark of
Hymns Ancient & Modern Ltd
13A Hellesdon Park Road, Norwich,
Norfolk NR6 5DR, UK

The authors acknowledge with thanks the help of Banxia Software
for the use of Decision Explorer to organize ideas.

British Library Cataloguing in Publication data

A catalogue record for this book is available
from the British Library

978 0 334 05547 1

Typeset by Manila Typesetting Company
Printed and bound by CPI Group (UK) Ltd

Contents

What Is Leadership?

The concept of leadership can be a controversial one within churches, for various reasons. Some people believe that churches are poorly led and need better leadership drawing upon the insights of industry and business schools. Others argue that such thinking is contrary to the Church's ethos and theology, so should be resisted at all costs. And yet others have applied leadership ideas to their own church experience with a multiplicity of outcomes and programmes for how churches should proceed. This chapter seeks to explore our understanding of the art of leadership and how some of the ideas about this can make a positive contribution to understanding what it is to lead in a church. In particular, we identify leadership as an action and not a role, which has significant implications for how we should think about church leadership.

Introduction

Have you ever heard people complaining of a lack of leadership? If so, what exactly was missing? Was it a charismatic figure that everyone could feel inspired by? Was it someone who negotiated well on behalf of their church, or their particular interest group within the church? Was it someone who made everything fit together, so that you knew why your work mattered? Someone who could express a clear image of where everyone was trying to go and what they were trying to achieve? Or someone who made everyone feel good about being part of the church or the group within the church that they were working in at the time? Leadership is used to cover all these needs, so we will start with a definition that may help us to agree what we are talking about.

Leadership is imagining, willing and driving, and thereby making something happen which was not going to happen otherwise. It is not following instructions on pieces of paper or the latest theory pronounced by a leadership guru. (Fineman, Sims and Gabriel, 2010, p. 85)

That definition is a few years old now, and the word that needs updating is 'making'. The idea that leaders make something happen feels outdated with the progress that has been made in thinking about chaos and complexity (Wheatley, 2006). Now we would say 'enabling'. By the end of this book we will also have qualified what is meant by 'willing', and even more 'driving', but we still find this definition helpful because it is all about activities, not about role or position. The activities do not need to be conducted by a person officially designated as 'leader'. Note also that there are several different activities here. Leadership needs an act of imagination, the vision to see what might be brought about. It requires will power, the capacity to stay with a project and not be deflected or forget what you are trying to achieve. Finally it requires driving, the capacity to take things through to conclusion.

The second half of the definition takes us into some ideas about what leadership is not. It is not about doing things because a trainer told you to do them on a leadership development programme, or because a self-appointed leadership guru says you should do them. Those who lead do not always respond well to leadership development; it may just annoy them. A theme of this book is that there are many different ways of being involved in leadership within churches, many different activities that need to be done, many different styles in which those activities could be done, and this requires more subtlety than the average development programme can handle. Leadership only works well if a number of different people with different qualities work together to make it happen.

Leadership as panacea

Leadership has been bedevilled by being seen as a panacea, in churches as in other organizations. If you have a problem that resists definition, the current fashion is to dub it a 'leadership problem'. Leadership is the new alchemy, the activity that is supposed to turn all to gold. Continual disappointment does not seem to cure us of this; how many people have complained of a lack of leadership, and then complained even more when they are given leadership that turns out not to be the kind, or to lead them in the direction, that they wanted?

This demand for a panacea has been fuelled from the supply side by a large number of authors and trainers who have recognized a good living when they have seen one. If there are plenty of people who are anxious about the quality of leadership, and about how to make it better, what an opportunity for anyone who has held a senior post to make some money after their redundancy. Something of this secular development is also seen in churches as the number of consultancy offerings on how to lead churches continues to grow.

Beyond heroes, villains and fools

In our culture we are very inclined to put single labels on people as if that told us all we needed to know about them, as is illustrated by the tabloid newspapers every day. For example, at the time of the banking crisis in 2008 onwards, in the UK politicians and bankers were widely labelled as 'greedy', churches were accused of 'not giving leadership', and public sector workers were routinely described as lazy and bureaucratic. There is also a tendency to build leaders up in the public imagination, only to tear them down again later. Why?

Public agendas are set by people who need to gather interest in what they are saying. Journalists and bloggers both need readers, and to gain and maintain those readers they need stories. There is no story in saying, 'This person has been doing a really good job and continues to do so.' You need a narrative arc, an account of improvement or deterioration, and your story will be more interesting if it obeys the principles of a good drama. It needs a plot with, as Shakespeare put it, 'heroes, villains and fools'.

One of the major newspapers in the UK publishes profiles of successful business leaders. We asked a senior journalist on this newspaper why they did this when they knew that it did not reflect reality, when they knew that the achievements they were talking about were never the result of just one person's work. 'Yes,' was the reply, 'we know the world does not work like that, but it makes a good story to frame it in terms of one individual's efforts; it is what our readers expect.' Television programmes on leadership are equally dominated by individualistic, heroic storytelling, which is a long way from most people's experience of good leadership.

Many of the books on leadership are built around case studies of important, successful and preferably well-known leaders. In order to write those case studies the authors collude with the myth of the solitary leadership genius, working their own magic to make wonderful things happen, although a helpful critique of this approach can be found in Brown (2014). The leaders concerned are often happy to go along with this. After all, it justifies their salaries and builds their reputation. The trouble is that this gives a distorted view of how leadership works. Instead, wherever we see leadership working well, while there may be some remarkable individuals involved, there are also others who are enabling those individuals to do what they do best, who are equally necessary in enabling leadership to succeed.

Leadership, generosity and humility

Much work in this field has shown that qualities such as generosity and humility are important in good leadership, the leadership that actually makes a difference (Collins, 2001). At the same time, we notice that models of heroic, individualistic leadership which are now 20 or 30 years out of date seem to be reaching heights of popularity in church circles (for example in the Church of England reports *Talent Management for Future Leaders: A New Approach*, 2014, p. 4; and *From Anecdote to Evidence*, 2014, p. 10). How ironic it would be if, just as the leadership world was beginning to catch up with some of the qualities traditionally admired in faith-based communities, the church was heading off in the opposite direction in her concern to adopt what are imagined to be the latest management ideas.

One of us worked some years back for what should have been an outstanding department. Most of its members went on to establish international reputations, and it is still talked about as having been a hotbed of talent. Its net effect, however, was minimal. When people look back in puzzlement, the commonest way of understanding this is that the formal leader of the group, admired and loved for his charisma, intelligence and humour, also lacked generosity and humility. Those who are effective in leadership are often people who are willing to give without counting the cost, and who are sufficiently confident in themselves not to need their egos boosted by the continuous admiration of others. Leadership, like love, works best when you give it away.

In the Orthodox Jewish tradition, Moses is referred to as the most humble man who ever lived. He had the most contact with God, and yet remained humble, and he lived the paradox. Related to this is the Hasidic saying: 'Everyone must have two pockets. In the right pocket one must keep the words *for my sake the world was created* and in the left *I am but dust and ashes*.'

It should be noted that humble leaders do not necessarily make 'nice' decisions. Humility has nothing to do with only giving soft answers, or trying to please everyone. Humility is to do with not having ego needs that get in the way of what you are doing.

Leadership as activity or role

Our definition of leadership, above, is framed in terms of activity rather than role. This is an important distinction because phrases such as 'being promoted to a leadership position' are frequently heard. Of course some positions give you more opportunities to exercise leadership than others. However, no place in which we have seen leadership working well has relied solely on senior people for leadership. Effective leadership relies on a collaboration between several different people with different qualities. If leadership is expected to come only from the top, this is a recipe for the senior person (very often, in a church, the minister) to feel isolated, overloaded and ineffective. The role of the senior person in any well-functioning organization is to bring together the leadership activities of others and to contribute to them, but it is *not* to be 'the leader'. This is one of the most pernicious myths from bad leadership teaching that we hope will be exploded for readers of this book.

Another way of considering this is to think about the difference between leadership and leading, the noun and the verb. The noun suggests something more static, more of a role, more to do with the expectations that people have of the leader and the rights and responsibilities that the leader carries. The verb suggests an activity which may be done by several people together, which may be passed from person to person when appropriate, which may be done in several different ways and which requires quite a combination of different activities to make it happen. Our view is that the noun 'leadership' needs to be treated with care. It has misled as often as it has helped, and it is one of those words whose lack of clear meaning only confuses. This is serious because the verb, 'leading', represents a fundamentally important human activity, one without which most other activities are less effective than they could be.

Leading in context

To what extent is leadership generic? Will the person who is good at leading a regiment, or a multinational company, be good at leading a church or chairing a meeting of the church council? The debate has gone to and fro in leadership studies. In the 1980s and

1990s there was a tendency to believe that leadership was porta-
ble, and that someone who could lead in one context could trans-
fer that ability to another context. Senior military and commercial
figures were appointed as the chief executives of health trusts, or
charities, or government agencies. Rarely were these transfers successful. Very often what started out with hubris ended in tears, as
the new recruits found that they simply did not understand the
complexity of the situations into which they had been recruited.

The importance of context comes from at least two sources.
First, it is difficult to be part of offering leadership in an organization that you do not understand. Without wishing to get bogged
down in the organization's history ('we tried that in 1992 and it
did not work then, so we won't do it again . . .'), those involved
in leading need to understand enough of the story of their organization to know what everyone is talking about, and they may also
need to know where the bodies are buried. Second, there are ways
of leading that are simply inappropriate to the organization that
you are in. If you are running a prison, you may be able to give
orders and to assume that you know the best way forward. You
cannot do the same if you are running a voluntary organization,
where your fellow members believe they have expertise that you
should value, and where they have the option of walking away
if they do not feel involved or committed to the direction of the
organization.

Making something happen which was not going to happen otherwise is never an innocent activity. By implication, you are also
stopping things happening which would have happened if you had
minded your own business. There may well be those who feel they
have gained from what you are doing, and there will be those who
feel they have lost from it. There will be those who wish you had
enabled something else to happen, or even nothing, in preference
to what you actually did. If everybody is happy with your leadership activities then either they have not understood you or you
have done nothing!

In churches there may be a feeling that, if we only tried hard
enough, we could, in the words that used to feature in the Church
of England's intercessions, 'seek the common good'. This is a
mirage. We can seek the good. We can seek one another's good.

But 'the common good' implies a dangerously depoliticized view of the world in which people do not have genuinely competing interests. Those engaged in leadership will need to be able to develop the organization's story in ways that are exciting, so that members will join in with enabling something to happen despite knowing that it is not for their own immediate, personal good.

The art of leadership

Leadership activity has been likened to pottery. Enabling things to happen as a leader is an artistic activity, but there is also a body of knowledge, a science, without which it is not likely to work very well. Understanding the chemistry of the materials for pottery is an essential stepping stone to being able to pot, but it is not sufficient, and once you have reached an acceptable level of quality, further understanding will not make you a better potter.

The same applies to leadership. Many people have puzzled as to why we do not seem to get much further with being able to make hard scientific statements about leadership, particularly when the public interest and funding available for studying it are relatively strong.

Grint (2000) suggests that this is because we have been studying it in the wrong way. The methodology and epistemology for studying art and science are quite different. Much of the study of leadership has treated it as a science; can we identify the elements of it? Can we add a little more of something to the mixture and get the reaction we want? These might be appropriate if we were researching chemistry or a physical science, but they are inappropriate to researching an art. We will make progress when we call it by its proper name, and treat it as an art.

Grint has taken this further, and suggested four different leadership arts:

1 *Philosophical art*, which is setting the identity of an organization. Who are we? What sort of organization are we? What are the stories that we tell about ourselves? Our past? Our future? What do we tell potential recruits about ourselves? What are

we here for? This art of leadership requires someone to focus
on the identity of the organization, which members and potential members alike will expect to show some continuity, but
also some development.

2 *Fine art*, which is designing a future vision for an organization.
What is this organization trying to do? What might its future
activity and achievement look like? This requires someone to
focus on designing an attractive future for the organization.

3 *Martial art*, which is making sure that everything works. There
is no point in being clear about what kind of organization you
are, and having a wonderful vision, if the photocopier isn't
working and nobody knows what is happening when. This
requires someone who can engage in the continuously needed
activity of organizing, who is prepared to devote themselves to
keeping chaos at bay. This is perhaps the most underrated of
leadership arts. A candidate for ordination was heard to say
that he had been a churchwarden for some years, but wanted
to contribute more spiritually. This is a typical undervaluing
of Grint's martial art, as if there were something lesser about
making things work well. It is often assumed that anybody can
do this, but a look around churches will show that very often
nobody is doing it, with disastrous consequences.

4 *Performance art*, which is the use of symbols and charisma to
excite people to action. Who can raise the energy levels? Who
can make people feel good about being part of the organization?
Who can attract people? This is a much better recognized leadership art, and much more generally valued – possibly overvalued.
Charisma for its own sake can be very damaging. Charisma, still
often the first leadership quality that people think of, is destructive and dangerous if it is not accompanied by other leadership
arts. If you do not know what sort of organization you are running, if you do not have a vision for where you are going, and if
you keep messing up the organization, charisma may just make
people angry, as they are continually disappointed.

Our argument is that, for leadership to take place, all four of these
need to be present. It does not much matter which of them is done
by whom, or which of them is done by the most senior person, but

they are unlikely all to be done by the same person; nobody has that much bandwidth.

This list has been extended by Sims (2010) to reflect three other arts that are often seen working in leadership:

1 *Poet in residence.* Poets choose their words with singular skill and effectiveness, and the ability to find exactly the right word for the moment can be an important contributor to leadership. All of the leadership arts described above can be made more effective if there is a poet in residence to 'give well-crafted sets of words which can be used by themselves or others to express identity, vision, organization and charisma'.

2 *Contemplative art.* This is the art of being aware of who you are and what qualities you bring, and being prepared to stay with what is, stepping out of the action framework. It was well described by the Chief Operating Officer of a major financial company, as follows:

It is a matter first of looking at the task, saying 'What kind of leadership do we need here?' And that is as much about deciding what we do not need. Too much leadership is like too much of anything else – it just makes you feel a bit sick. Makes the company fat too, and the last thing (my company) needs is to store its energy round its waist!

3 *Narrative art.* This is in some ways like the philosophical art, which often operates by telling a story about identity. However, there is more to it than the development of the church's identity. There is also a sense in which, if we exercise leadership, we will make appearances in the stories of others. For some people, the meaning of life is the extent to which you write yourself into the stories of others. In addition, there is a narrative art in being aware that you are a story as well as a storyteller. You will be developing your own story of yourself, writing the next chapter of your life, and you will be offering a story of yourself that is passed on around the organization. Recall any organization you have joined; many of the stories you were told in the first few days concerned particular people in leadership roles,

how they behaved under different conditions, and thus how you should understand their characters. 'Giving a testimony' exemplifies this well. An analysis of narrative art in a church context can be found in Roberts (2014).

We would want to add one more art to this list, which we will call the *art of problem construction*, or 'dilemma-flipping' (Johansen, 2009). Who decides what problems are worth paying attention to, spending time and resources on? And do they craft problems in such a way that they are soluble and positive, rather than depressing and not inviting action? We shall return to this in the summary of this chapter, and we will come back to how all these arts are exercised, or not, in churches later in this book.

Leadership phases

There are many other ways in which different kinds of leadership activity can be seen to be needed. For example, in the different phases of a project, different leadership activities are called for.

Any new project should start with a nurturing phase, where people get to know each other, work out together what they are trying to do, define the problems they are going to work on, and look to see what resources are available to them. Leadership in this phase needs to be quite allowing and gentle. The pace needs to be kept slow, as many of these activities fail most often because they have been rushed or skipped. Many groups do not spend enough time working out what they are really trying to do, defining the problem they are working on. This is because those who were exercising leadership were trying to make things happen too early, rather than dwelling long enough with the phase of understanding the problem. That such over-anxiety should be found in churches perhaps ought to be surprising.

Commonly, the next phase is where people are coming forward with proposed actions, debating how to go about doing the needful. This is the exciting stage for many action-orientated people, and at this stage there ought to be some conflicts that need to be resolved. If this is not the case, the energy being generated is probably not as high as it should be. Leadership needs to recognize that not every-body can have their ideas adopted, that there will need to be win-ners and losers, and that the energy must not be damped down by trying to please everybody. Losers need to be looked after.

This leads to a phase of doing, the phase where the work of the project happens. Leadership at this phase is about organizing and maintaining, enabling people to see where they are in the activity and assuring them that they are making progress, or letting them know if they are not. The martial art of leadership is crucial here, along with maintaining motivation.

We now reach the peak of the project, where the objective is achieved. This carries its own excitement, and may need little lead-ership. However, many involved in church leadership find difficulty in finishing activities off, and have trouble energizing themselves to do the boring bits at the end, once they can see that their main objective has been achieved. So leadership at this stage may require us to honour those who can focus on the completion of tasks.

Finally there is the celebration of having achieved what was intended. Whether this is a party or a service, this is one of the most underrated phases. The evidence is that the project team that does not celebrate its achievements has increasing trouble achiev-ing again. Its members are left feeling flat or even exploited. David once worked in a group of project teams and, like his colleagues, was not too sad when the best party animal left. He had never made much contribution to the substance of the projects. It was only later that they realized how important this person had been for leading the celebrations.

The implications of this are that we may need to involve more people in leadership because the different phases require such dif-ferent qualities. The minister who believes that she or he is the right person to lead throughout this process is worryingly deluded.

The aesthetics of leadership

Leadership attempts often fail, not because people disagree with the directions of those who wish to lead them, but because they look at the would-be leaders and think 'yuck'. One helpful way of thinking about leadership is the notion of 'leading beautifully'. Ladkin (2008) points out that to consider anything other than art aesthetically is relatively alien to western ways of thinking; but then, as we have been saying, leadership is best thought of as a set of arts. As she says:

> Leading beautifully speaks to a quality of being – one honed through the development of self-mastery, and quickened through the congruence of one's acts with their 'measured' expression. It also alerts us to the possibility of a leader's goals being directed towards the best of human purposes.

Nothing there that most involved in church leadership would want to argue with. All through Ladkin's work, the idea of leading beautifully requires those involved in leadership not to be individually beautiful, which will be a relief to many of us, but to embody and enact what they are trying to achieve in leadership. In this approach, the end never justifies the means; the means must be beautiful too.

The importance of followership

Leadership implies that someone is following, and the role of the follower has attracted increasing interest in recent years, as illustrated by Goffee and Jones' (2006) book title, *Why Should Anyone Be Led by You?* Most of the discussion of followership has been based on old-fashioned ideas of leadership, whereby a heroic 5 per cent of the population are 'natural leaders' and the rest are naturally followers. We have been unable to find any good evidence for this implicitly fascist view of the world, and it is completely out of keeping with everything else we have been saying about leadership. There are so many different contributions to make to leadership that almost everybody will make one of them some time.

However, there is a considerable art in being a good follower, and our picture of leadership is that at any particular time you need the appropriate people stepping forward to offer leadership while other people, whose leadership gifts are not the most important at that moment, step back for a while and exercise followership (Kellerman, 2008). Good followership is the kind that supports the leadership activities going on at the time, perhaps as a critical friend, but never with the kind of sullen grudge that leeches energy out of those trying to enable something to happen which was not going to happen otherwise. Sadly, the possibility that some followers become energy sinks for those currently trying to move things forward is not unknown in churches.

Beyond the heroic and the controlling

The world has moved on from ideas about leadership as being exercised only by extraordinarily talented and very unusual individuals. Such people may be part of leadership teams, but fortunately we are not dependent on them. To some extent the reverse is true: we have long known that teams of highly talented people often produce quite mediocre or even dreadful results (known in the organizational literature as 'the Apollo syndrome'). Heroes can be as much a liability as an asset, as some of the great heroes that led the banking industry for the years leading up to 2008 illustrated. Excessive admiration is destructive. Malcolm Gladwell (2008) has a very good chapter on how Korean Airways decreased its accident rate significantly by reducing the awe in which airline pilots were held by their subordinates. Innumerable failures in health, business and politics can be attributed to people being seen as heroes, having their propaganda believed by their subordinates and, worse still, themselves, and thus believing that they should not deprive the world of their own dominance. As Jesus tells his listeners: 'Woe to you when everyone speaks well of you' (Luke 6.26). This is true for many reasons, including the probability that they are too frightened or too lazy to give you the more rounded picture.

The need for a leader to feel in control usually has more to do with insecurity on the part of the controlling person than with the needs of the organization. In most organizations, it is hard for those at the top to be well in touch with what is happening on the ground. The more uncertain we are, the more we may be prone to feeling that all would be well if only everybody else did what we would do if we were in their situation, or, in other words, if they were under our control.

This may seem obvious, but it needs to be said because the tradition of trusting heroes and controlling others needs to be seen for the dangerous and impoverished authoritarianism (or dependency – this is sometimes forced on leaders by followers) that it is. It keeps cropping up, for example in language such as 'management's right to manage', and it is always potentially destructive.

Distributed leadership

An important development in leadership thinking is the idea that leadership may be distributed among members of an organization. Raelin (2003) has talked about effective organizations as being *leaderful*. In other words, there are leaders all over the place. This does not imply chaos, or that all are equal, or that decisions do not need to be made. Instead it means that, under the complexity and rate of change that are features of the world as we know it, we require many people to be involved in leadership.

Many churches are weighed down with activities that have been set up to meet a need at a particular time, but were then not closed down when the time ceased to be right. In the same way, many people start exercising leadership but find it much more difficult to step back and let someone else lead when the time is right. The more embattled you are, the more you may feel that you should carry on bearing the leadership burden and not pass it on until the difficulties have been dealt with. This is an example of how dangerous it can be for people to feel too strong a sense of responsibility.

Implicit in this is the idea that leadership is too important to be left to leaders. The organizations that we see adapting quickly and effectively are the ones that invite leadership and responsibility from members throughout. The same activity tends to be called leadership when exercised by senior people and responsibility when exercised by more junior people.

Some of the metaphors used in church life may militate against ideas of distributed leadership. The hierarchical character of some churches does not help senior clergy to enable leadership by more junior members. Also, there are some very problematic words such as 'flock', not normally a collective noun for potential leaders.

In a movement that has created considerable interest in secular organizations, Robert Greenleaf (1977) introduced the idea of 'servant leadership'. Laub (2000, p. 23) defines servant leadership as the 'practice of leadership that places the good of those led over the self-interest of the leader . . . [and] promotes the valuing and the development of people . . . sharing the power and status for the common good of each individual, the total organization and those served by the organization'. This means that those engaged in leadership see it not as a badge of honour, as something that makes them superior to other people, but as an act of service to their co-workers. In this view of leadership leaders may not be thanked or appreciated, at least at the time, and may not be rewarded with riches and fame for what they do. Indeed they might end up as martyrs, but their leadership is still offered in order to enable something to happen which was not going to happen otherwise.

We know that in churches it is easy for servant leadership to start well and gradually lose any visible link to being a servant. *Servus servorum dei*, 'the servant of the servants of God', is one of the titles of the Pope, but for some of those served by some Popes it has an ironic ring. We will come back to the notion of the leader who washes his followers' feet. A number of articles applying servant leadership to churches can be found in Jones (2016). The concept of the 'servant' suggests someone who does something *for* you, and we agree with the argument of Wells (2015) that this is a less helpful emphasis, in faith and life, than to think of someone who does something *with* you.

Isaacs (1999) and his colleagues (Senge, Scharmer, Jaworski and Flowers, 2005) have given 'dialogue' the specific meaning of people thinking together. There are times when people seem so close in their collaboration that the notion of one person talking and another listening does not capture the experience. The model that Isaacs uses is of networked computers, where the combined power of several machines working together is used to work with complex problems. The machines relate too closely to be able to say what work was done by which machine. Occasionally an inter-action between people can feel like that, where the understanding between them is so good that it no longer feels like one person producing a statement and other people responding to it, but like a co-production.

When this happens, it would be impossible to say which of the parties to the interaction was responsible for any new ideas or any progress made. This makes for a form of leadership so distributed that we do not even know who within the network can be cred-ited with what. This is highly valued by, for example, Investec, a major investment bank, as a way of working. It depends on the creation of a high level of trust, but if this can be achieved in an investment bank is it really so unreasonable to think that a church might manage it?

It seems to us that the parables in the Gospels operate in a way very akin to dialogue. In many cases the interpretation is not given, and the hearers seem to be expected to think together with Jesus, to understand beyond the literal content of the words, and to take meaning well beyond the verbal expression. This also reflects dia-logue in the level of trust that Jesus put in his listeners to think with him.

The persistence of heroic leadership

One of our colleagues went on the Senior Management Programme at one of the top US business schools, where the teaching about leadership was all about how to be the heroic, individual leader, with none of the insights that have been added since about 1980. Sadly this is not surprising. The people who teach such courses are not the top researchers in the field, because the researchers and thought leaders would never spend their time running a develop-ment programme. Instead, they are charismatic, likeable people on very short contracts, who need to receive good feedback on their course evaluation forms in order to get the next contract. The temptation to give the audience what it wants rather than what it might need must be massive. When their audience consists of a group of senior managers whose employers are prepared to spend big money to have them developed, the message that they are a group of really heroic people who are worth both their high salaries and huge development costs is always likely to go down well with them, and produce a good score for the teacher. Hence the persistence of the myth of heroic leadership.

Much fiction is based around heroic individual leaders, whether they are heroic for good or ill. For example, in the hugely popular *West Wing*, which was apparently the preferred viewing of Tony Blair and his aides during his premiership, President Bartlett is portrayed as a heroic fighter for good values and supporter of those who are downtrodden, as well as being a polymath, having superhuman levels of energy, and being a kind and committed family man. He expects to be able to understand all the major issues of state sufficiently to be the person who makes the decision about them. Occasionally he allows one of his aides to remind him of some value that he holds which risks being breached, although he may warn them that they are close to 'crossing the line'. But there is never any idea that he might step back and let someone else lead in their areas of expertise, which creates a crisis when his daughter is kidnapped and he temporarily releases the reins. This is a classic presentation of heroic leadership, and the programme invites those who watch it to imagine themselves in the shoes of this all-seeing, all-competent president. It is all done so well that few notice the very unhelpful model of leadership that it is promoting.

Learning to lead

We have many ways of learning to contribute to leadership, of which leadership development programmes form a relatively minor one. Leadership is as much about attitude as anything, and that is not the kind of thing you learn under someone else's control, whether in a seminar room or on an outdoor management development programme.

The dominant way of learning leadership is by apprenticeship. You work alongside someone who is involved in leadership, you watch what they do, you help them with parts of it, they take care of your learning and mentor you, and gradually you learn the lessons from them sufficiently to be able to operate as a leader in your own right. The implication is that there is a heavy responsibility on the apprentice master or mistress. There is every likelihood that your apprentices will learn your bad habits as well as your good ones, and the things that you do because you have always done them as well as the things you do deliberately.

Similarly to this, people learn leadership by mimicry. There was an old friend and colleague of ours who was widely admired for his leadership abilities. He was charismatic, witty, clever, and people would follow him anywhere. Every now and then in a meeting you would hear one of his junior colleagues come up with a phrase which you knew came from the boss. The real give-away was that they would sometimes say these phrases in his Yorkshire accent. This was not conscious on their part, and they did not think that his leadership effectiveness was caused by his accent. It was because they were learning leadership through mimicry, by which we mean that they were method acting their boss, they were trying to be him and to act him out, and in so doing they were not distinguishing between those of his qualities that they thought were key and others. Mimicry does not distinguish.

Bob Johansen (2009) talks about the need for rapid prototyping in learning leadership. He says that people should aim to 'fail early, fail often and fail cheaply'. We do not learn by reflecting deeply on how and why things work, especially in such action-oriented activities as leadership. We only learn when we try something and see what happens. At the same time, most of us have seen people who are not too good at deciding what to try next; more of a theoretical base helps you to think what rapid prototyping experiment would be worth trying next, and may accelerate the learning from prototyping.

Finally, in learning to lead, there is the question of how people learn to let go. Letting go, trusting those you are working with, is one of the hardest lessons to learn for those coming into leadership. This is true in most professions; the engineer trying to develop leadership activities finds herself perpetually leaning over junior members of the profession advising them how to do the technical work when this is no longer her role. This is natural because she has been an expert in that technical work; she knows how to do it, and knows what she has achieved at the end of the day, both of which satisfactions are harder to achieve in leadership.

A few leadership irritations

Leadership may mean giving away the credit for your achievements. Those engaged in counselling often find that they need to let their clients take ownership of their own solutions in order not to create dependency, and this happens frequently for leaders. For the development of those around you, it may be important not to claim ownership of achievements that you could fairly claim. Robert Winship Woodruff, the long-serving CEO of Coca-Cola, had a sign on his desk that said, 'There is no limit to what a man can do or where he can go if he does not mind who takes the credit.' Or as Indira Gandhi put it, 'My grandfather once told me that there are two kinds of people: those who work and those who take the credit. He told me to try to be in the first group; there was less competition there.'

Church leadership is bedevilled by key words that are heard from those in the private sector, and taken too uncritically. The idea that successful leadership entails a 'bias for action' can be traced back to a book by Peters and Waterman (1982) called *In Search of Excellence*. Although many of their 'excellent' companies have since gone out of business, the book's influence remains, and one of their mottos is the 'bias for action'. In the context of their time, the suggestion of not getting bogged down in bureaucracy was no doubt valuable, and it is ironic that churches have mostly increased their bureaucracy since then. But their motto has frequently been used to short-circuit discussions that need to happen. As Sull (2010) puts it:

A dysfunctional bias for action is endemic among 'take-charge' or 'gung-ho' executives who excel at getting things done, but dread the open-ended discussions required to understand situations where complexity, ambiguity, and incomplete data preclude easy answers. To avoid this discomfort, they bypass discussions to make sense and dive right into making choices or working out the details of implementation. By jumping too quickly to discussions on how to take the hill, however, these teams often end up attacking the wrong hill.

We should also not uncritically accept the idea that being involved in leadership is something to be desired, and that those with leadership roles will have made bids for those roles. The experience of those involved in leading is often that others will have pushed them forward into leadership, and will also have expectations about what that leadership should consist of and what activities they should engage in to do it 'properly'. Taking up leadership, and making choices about how it should be exercised, can be something done by the followers to the leaders as much as the other way round.

Summary and conclusion

Our emphasis in this chapter has been that much of the misunderstanding of leadership has come from confusing the role with the action. 'Leadership roles' are taken to mean seniority, whether or not the person engages in leadership – and there are plenty of examples from all sectors where people achieve 'leadership roles' by avoiding leadership action. We see it as far more useful to think of leadership as the activity of enabling something to happen which was not going to happen otherwise, and contributions to this activity may be made by many people. Perhaps this should not be a surprise to anyone familiar with St Paul's metaphor of the church as a body, with all its parts being important and needing each other in order to function. So the emphasis on leadership as contribution is one that we might want to make for any organization, but is almost self-evidently appropriate for a church. By implication, this works when feet do what feet do best and the liver does what it does best. As Einstein said, 'Everyone is a genius. But if you judge a fish on its ability to climb a tree, it will spend its whole life believing it's stupid.'

Questions

1   Think of a time when you have been led well. What was so good about that leadership? Have you been able to use some of what was good about that leadership in your leadership of others?
2   Which of the leadership arts do you think are the most natural ones for you to exercise? Which ones are not so much your home ground, although you could learn to do them? And which ones would it be best for you to enable someone else to perform?
3   In what ways do you think leadership in your church should be different from, for example, a regiment, or a hospital, or a private company?

2

Leading the Stories and
Storying the Leading

This chapter takes the idea of leadership as a set of arts and explores it further by setting out the place of storytelling within churches in the light of the 'narrative turn' in recent thinking. Increasingly it is recognized in the world of business and other organizations that the notion of the 'heroic leader' has failed and a better understanding is needed of how the process of leading actually works. One of the ways in which the relationship between leading and following can be worked out is through the stories that are told (and not told) by communities and individuals. We explore the basis of this thinking and how it might help churches in their development of a better understanding of leading in a relational way. We will take this under four headings:

- Leadership and stories: human beings live out storied lives. Leadership can participate in those stories.
- Different contributions to leading the story: this is not often done by one person alone, and it is not only done from the top. Seniority can be useful in leadership, but it is not the same thing as leadership.
- Hierarchies and control of stories: control is not leadership.
- Stories and the love of small things: leadership in love.

Leadership and stories

In this chapter we offer an understanding of leadership as story-telling, following the 'narrative turn' which has characterized both the social sciences and theology in the last 25 years or so (Denzin, 1996; Ganzevoort, 2011). We shall discuss storytelling and narrative without getting hung up on the distinctions sometimes made between them, which we do not need here. A narrative approach is one that looks at how stories are being told. Leadership studies have lagged well behind in their understanding of the relationship between leading and stories (Denning, 2011a; Mead, 2014), and this has both reinforced and been reinforced by the idea that 'leadership' is a tainted concept, often used as a euphemism for trying to control others rather than for understanding or enabling what anyone else is doing. While he was Archbishop of Canterbury, Rowan Williams spoke of how there were 'several Churches of England' with their different stories – for further suggestions on this, see Woodhead (2013). In the context of this 'mixed economy' of ecclesial organization Williams observed that the mission of the Church is 'finding out what God is doing and joining in' (Williams, 2003). In a similar vein we would argue that the task of leadership in churches is to find out what narratives God is unfolding and join in the storytelling.

Talking about how people work together always involves using a metaphor for the human person. Older work on leadership views people in ways such as the economic (making 'rational' self-orientated decisions), the social (making decisions that maximize their membership in the groups around them), or the self-actualizing (seeking to develop themselves according to their own potential); it may even view people as sheep. The different metaphors carry their own implications: for example, the rational economic metaphor implies that people are not altruistic, and also that they are capable of complex calculations about what is best for themselves. (See Alvesson and Spicer (2011) for other ways in which leadership metaphors shape organizational sensemaking, and Roberts (2000) and (2008) for the use of metaphors in church ministry.)

We believe that we can gain more light on church and leadership by considering the person as *homo narrans narratur*, that is, both a storyteller and a story (Christie and Orton, 1988; Weick, 1995). We tell stories and at the same time we ourselves are a story. We are continuously constructing the next part of the story that is ourselves. We work out our plotlines, introduce new characters into our story, lose the plot, do things to liven up our own stories as we go along. As Hardy (1968) put it:

> We dream in narrative, we daydream in narrative, remember, anticipate, we hope, despair, believe, doubt, plan, review, criticize, build, learn, hate and love by narrative.

This chapter opens up a theme that will continue throughout this book about the value of a storytelling view of leadership in churches. One of the things we know about ourselves as a species is that we tell stories, we develop our own stories, and we enthusiastically consume stories told by others. In church, we hear stories from the Bible and are invited in sermons to think about our own story, who we are in relationship with God and with others. We are challenged to consider the totality of our story, to death and beyond. Jesus is recorded in the Gospels as having frequently told stories, using parables and talking to people about their stories and how they saw those developing in the future. A narrative approach to leadership would seem to be the natural approach for his followers to take, and has been explored in biblical studies (for example Wright, 1992) and theology (for example Loughlin, 1996; Smith, 2009, 2013).

When leadership happens, people are writing themselves into others' stories (Edwards, 2000). If you enable something to happen you must be making at least a guest appearance in the stories of the other people involved. We all take some of our sense of effectiveness and personhood from believing that we have had some part in other people's stories, and this is one of the motivations for leading.

In everyday conversation there are several different ways in which the word 'story' is used. For example, there is the sense of 'just a story', in contrast to 'the truth'. The implication is either that a good story is a way of blinding people to the truth or that storytelling is a kind of second-order activity, inferior to other 'rational' forms of discourse as a way of conveying what we want to say. Of course, storytelling is always selective. If someone asks you to tell them what sort of day you have had you will tell a story. It is impossible to tell them everything that has happened; there is not enough time and they will not attend for long enough. In order to keep their attention and to help them reach the conclusions about you and your day that you would like them to reach, you make choices about what to include and exclude. Similarly, when a colleague enquires of another minister or a bishop asks a priest about how things are going in the church, the answer can only be a story, and it can only be the story as understood by the teller. It will usually be their truth; there is no reason to suppose that people deliberately mislead any more when they are telling stories than when they are giving supposedly objective answers to census returns.

Even when data are given in statistical form, any attempt to read them or to talk about them will immediately turn them into narrative form. The role of the church treasurer includes responsibility for telling a story about tables of figures which other members may find boring or incomprehensible – to take the accounts and to use them to tell a story. This story will give them a meaning, and that meaning is chosen by the treasurer. Steve Denning illustrates this process of choice with the example of the *Titanic*. It would have been possible, he points out, for the newspaper headline the day after the sinking to have said '700 people safely reach New York' (Denning, 2011a), but that was not the choice of meaning made by the press. When conflict occurs in the Middle East, it is quite common to see almost exactly the same story (coming from the same newsfeeds) in different newspapers, but with headlines that blame different parties. We frame data according to what we think others should pay attention to. Sometimes this may be for our own benefit, but more commonly we will see it as our way of helping the other person to see through to the core points of what we are talking about. Boje (2012) uses the word 'antenarrative' for the resources that are available for storytelling (as in the example of the accounts) and 'narrative' for the story that gets created from them.

When data are presented statistically, this may be not an alternative to storytelling but a part of the storytelling. As Gearóid O'Crualaoich (2002) has commented, an important part of telling any story is the warranting of its reliability. In his case, working with Irish folk stories, a frequent warranting phrase is, 'It was a priest who told me . . . '. In current western culture our fashionable way of warranting a story is to give some statistics that we claim support it. The link between the statistics and the story being warranted may be distant, the logic may not bear close scrutiny, but it is expected that we should have some statistics as part of the narrative (for a careful use of this approach, see Woodhead, 2013). This can be part of an evidence-based approach to whatever we are doing; the statistics can be used to confirm that we are actually achieving what we are trying to achieve.

One of the characteristics of storytelling is that it handles complexity and ambiguity better than many other forms of discourse. Stories are usually told with a certain amount of redundancy, points that may not be relevant but may be interesting, the possibility of more than one outcome, some ambiguity about what are the central plot lines of the story and the essential actors. In addition, they are told with decorative flourishes, but part of the art of storytelling is to leave it unclear whether a particular statement is decorative or a load-bearing part of the narrative structure. It is typical of good storytelling that 'the dog that did not bark in the night' (Conan Doyle, 1893) could have been irrelevant until late in the story, when it emerges that it is doing part of the narrative work. Similarly, a joke may be introduced into a story to gauge the audience reaction to it, to test out their attitudes. If they react badly to it, the teller dismisses it as 'just a joke'. If they react well, it may be an area of further development later.

Also, discussion may take place through stories. In one church the minister was frequently surprised that when he laid out a series of options to the management committee the response was not a discussion of the merits and demerits of the choices but a series of stories adjacent to the proposals. His initial frustration was gradually replaced by a realization that this was how that community dealt with proposals for change, and also possibly how they held conversations. Storytelling was the form of discourse through which decisions were made.

The most memorable and influential stories invite the listener to participate by leaving some open questions as to what they mean and how they might be interpreted. Barthes (1974) speaks of 'readerly' and 'writerly' texts, where readerly means that you cast the other person into a relatively passive role where they read what you are saying, and writerly means that they are seen as active co-authors of the script. Both are possible when we are writing ourselves into others' stories. If our storytelling is readerly, they are less likely to get us wrong, because their interpretive contribution will be less, but they are also less likely to be led anywhere by us. If our leadership storytelling is writerly we may be misinterpreted and people may well not do what we want, but they are much more likely to do something as a result, because it will be *their* something; they have felt invited to participate in writing the story. Once again, the managerial desire to control is likely to make a church more predictable, if that is what you think a church should be! It is also likely to make it less active.

For example, in most cases, the parables of Jesus are reported without instructions on how they should be interpreted. Such a relaxation of control by the teller invites the listeners to become involved in what is being said, to think themselves into the story being told and to empathize with a character within it, thus making their own meaning out of what is being said. This is much more likely to produce learning that changes the learner than if the meaning of the parable were more tightly controlled by the teller. Storied communications are often an important part of effective leadership. Part of leading is to create a story around your organization. What kind of church is yours? Why would people want to be part of it? If they become part of this church, what can they expect to find themselves part of in a few years' time? What kind of story have they joined? How are they going to be invited to develop and grow if they join this story? If I become part of this church, what contribution can I make? Am I needed here? Finding a story that people can contribute to, in which they can find characters to become, and where they can help in making that story real, is one of the most inspiring ways to be led.

Parry and Hansen (2007) have argued that we all follow organizational stories as much as we follow people. 'People join with the narrative, rather than follow the leader.' In other words, one way of leading is to create and tell a story that people will wish to follow, or involve themselves with. Thinking about leading by story is important not because it is a new way of leading, but because it is what is happening anyhow, but its narrative quality has not been understood. Weick (1995) says that stories can be prophecies because they help people to make sense of what is going on, and people then act in accordance with that sense. So a believable story about how openness to different sexualities might threaten the doctrinal purity of a church can be enough to produce a fear-driven reaction, and the tightening of purity codes. If you do not tell the story of your church it will not remain untold. Someone else will do it for you. But you will have abrogated responsibility for the story, unless you support someone else to become the storyteller. Unconsidered, stories have a way of becoming the reality, as Weick argues. They will not remain untold, but may be told in a much less constructive way if you leave them to take their chances. Bennis and Nanus (2004) say that leaders are purveyors of hope. If the story is purveying hope, then the story is providing leadership (Parry, 2008).

Powerful stories do not get told and then forgotten. Stories get told and retold, sometimes through successive people but quite often by the same group of people, in the same way as families retell old stories about their family at gatherings ('Do you remember when Grandpa took his bicycle to pieces . . .?'). Parry (2008) argues that stories go on being told so long as each person has an understanding of the story that gives them hope for a better existence. Even if this role is a relatively minor one, this still gives a role from which they can act and from which they can try to make a contribution. Parry uses the example of the alternative stories that were provided by Martin Luther King and Malcolm X for the role of black people in the United States. At the time the two stories seemed to be equally powerful, but in hindsight Martin Luther King's story gave grounds for hope and roles for all participants, and it has survived and still influences American culture, whereas Malcolm X's more conflictual, less inclusive story of black power was less attractive and has disappeared (Parry, 2008). Perhaps we can look forward to a similar dissolving of the narratives of church decline that are so popular with some Christians.

Different contributions to leading the story

Whenever we see leadership working well, we can see contributions to it coming from several different places. This may then be reported in simplified stories in which the action centres on individually heroic leaders, whereas the reality is that those heroes need to work with others in order to be able to lead (Brown, 2014). Winston Churchill needed the political skills of Clemmie, his wife, as he reveals in his diaries. Nelson Mandela needed the wisdom and mentoring of Walter Sisulu, and similar examples can be found with all iconic leaders. There are too many kinds of work to be done in leadership for them all to be done by one person.

This means that the capacity for other people to offer something quite different, as suggested in 1 Corinthians 12, is important for any organization, and perhaps even more obviously so for the Body of Christ. As we observed in the previous chapter, Grint (2000) has pointed out that leadership requires the exercise of a number of different arts. You need someone who is good at the philosophical art of creating the story of the organization, someone who is good at the fine art of thinking about designing the future, someone who is good at the martial art of making sure that everything is working well, and someone who is good at the performance art of inspiring other people. There is absolutely no chance that one person will excel in all these arts, whatever they say on their application forms. Good leadership requires us to recognize what we are good at, and what we should invite others to do rather than attempting to do it all ourselves. Good leadership never means being good at everything, and anyone who thinks they are good at everything is too out of touch with reality to be a good leader. The traditional question at job interviews, 'Tell us your weaknesses', is often used as an opportunity to show that we are sufficiently verbally adept to turn weaknesses into strengths, but it should be taken more seriously. Anyone who does not think they have weaknesses will not appreciate their need to involve others in leadership. This is damaging anywhere, but even more so within a faith that is explicit about our not being able to do everything for ourselves.

This involves the recognition that, at different times and stages in the writing of any story, various people may need to come forward to lead the narrative process. So understanding how that works – when to speak up and when to keep silent – is crucial, and to do that successfully involves gifts of self-perception across a team. Boje (1991) has made the similar point that many stories are multi-authored. Particularly when the story is subject to telling and retelling, it can become a collaborative telling between several parties. For example, in churches, work organizations and families, there is a sociable process of telling long repeated stories together. Part of the way that the shared ownership of the story is symbolized is by the ability of different people to pick up the story, tell a few lines of it, and then be unconcerned when others interrupt to pick up the story, because they know that the story has been told often enough, and is sufficiently agreed, that the other person will still tell the story as they would have liked. This is a normal part of conversation, and works well so long as those in senior positions do not get taken up with their own importance and power, and start believing that they have the right or even the duty to control the story of the organization. Worst of all, perhaps, is when senior people invite others to join in a polyvocal story, and then suddenly reassert their authority. Being invited to offer an account of your church's story, and then being told by an authority figure that your version of the story was wrong, leads to demoralized, passive-aggressive followers.

Hierarchies and control of stories

It is easy to talk about leadership as if it were a universally acknowledged good, but there have recently been very useful studies of bad leadership such as that by Kellerman (2004). She says:

> Followers follow bad leaders not only because of their individual needs for safety, simplicity and certainty but also because of the needs of the group . . . Bad leaders often provide important benefits . . . maintain order, provide cohesion and identity . . .

Both the giving and the receiving of leadership are often connected with anxiety. If things are not going well, people may well reach for any source of certainty and clarity, and this often means that they seek 'strong' leadership, which tends to mean toxic leadership

(Lipman-Blumen, 2004). Situations of confusion and uncertainty have often been used by dictators to take control, as Hitler did in the demoralization of 1930s Germany, where many people were ready to vote for anyone who claimed to be able to make sense for them of what was going on. An emphasis on control as leadership dates back to the beginning of the twentieth century and the earliest leadership literature (Taylor, 1911), and innumerable studies have shown that it creates at least as many problems as it solves. Runciman (2013) calls the longing for control 'dictator envy', and shows that the view that a benevolent dictatorship is an effective form of governance can be shown to be quite wrong historically. However, it fits very well with anxiety, which is to be found in many churches; and it fits with an authoritarian personality type, which is also going to be represented in plenty of churches (and mosques, and temples, and humanist societies).

The problem with controlling leadership is that it is wasteful. It may have been adequate to the needs of early manufacturing, but it has been found to be of little value in a world where organizations need to make as much use as possible of the diverse abilities and knowledge of their staff, and where no one person can know enough, or be clever enough, to do all the thinking. Controlling leadership is comforting to those who wish to be told what to do, but it destroys people's opportunities to offer the best of their abilities and wisdom.

Controlling leadership may also be too ready to shield followers from the anxiety of the present moment. As Rahm Emanuel, Barack Obama's former White House Chief of Staff, said, 'You never let a serious crisis go to waste. And what I mean by that it's an opportunity to do things you think you could not do before.' Weick (1995) has been followed by many others in arguing that 'sensemaking and sensegiving are key parts of the leadership process' (Humphreys, Ucbasaran and Lockett, 2011). Helping people to make sense is a more effective way of leadership than telling them what to do, because it releases and employs more human potential.

Percy (2013) has argued that problems arise from regarding the Church as an organization, in which people work and need management, rather than as an institution, in which people have an occupation and need leadership. While we reach many of the same conclusions we do not think we need this distinction, because we do not think the managerialist approach works in any other kind of organization either. The managerial preoccupations of the last 30 years have been about how to deprofessionalize, how to turn work into a matter of measurable output, rather than being about the identity-related, long-term development of the effective professional. The prescriptions that are offered on innumerable courses (SMART objectives, continuous review and appraisal, payment by results, 360 degree feedback, etc.) may also be a way for people who are very well paid to disguise from their colleagues that they do not know what they are doing, and do not have any sense of professional pride or confidence in their actions (Scott, 2009). So long as they put plenty of these procedures in place, they hope they will be able to deflect any accusations of idleness or negligence. The speed with which they then adopt any new form of measurement they can find shows that the anxiety is still there. In other words, the behaviour that Percy says may be more appropriate to other organizations than to the Church is probably not appropriate anywhere. They are all examples of Kellerman's 'bad leadership' and Lipman-Blumen's 'toxic leaders'. The Church, like other charities, is vulnerable to offerings from many plausible, usually well-meaning but insufficiently critical consultants, who may not have had the time to keep up to date with more recent leadership research and thinking.

One of the most persistently misleading ways of thinking about leadership is to think of leadership 'traits'. What are the qualities of a good leader? Much early leadership research concerned itself with this question, but although it sounds perfectly sensible it has produced no reliable answers. The number of possible qualities of the good leader has simply gone on growing until it has become meaningless. The suggestion that, to be a good leader, you should be noticeably above or below the average height is, we think, a spoof, but almost everything else has been suggested. This continues: recently, emotional intelligence has been offered as another trait of good leaders. However, with all these traits we can find plenty of counter-examples, so that they are not useful in practice. Similarly we see the upholding of heroic models. 'If you want to be a leader, be more like Steve Jobs, or Winston Churchill, or Nelson Mandela, or Desmond Tutu, or (until about 2009) Tony Blair, or (until 2008) some of the CEOs of big banks.' Studying past leaders and then trying to imitate them has no track record of success, whereas the advice of Goffee and Jones (2006) to 'be yourself, but more so' is much better attested. Perhaps, like washing yourself in the River Jordan, this advice is too simple to be attractive (2 Kings 5.1–14).

Profiling, through the Myers–Briggs inventory or other psychometric testing, has become very popular, and it can be used well or badly. If it is used as a way of making a judgement about the suitability of an individual for a job, that is an abuse behind which lies the idea that there is a right set of characteristics for carrying out a job, and that we can measure who has those right characteristics. The appointment of the Revd Paul Flowers as Chairman of the Cooperative Bank was justified by psychometric testing, even though he knew little about banking and was unable to save his bank from disastrous decisions. He was later described by the Treasury Committee chairman, Andrew Tyrie, as 'psychologically unbalanced but psychometrically brilliant' (Connor, 2014). Apart from its unreliability, much of the past use of profiling has been based on a trait theory of leadership, which as we explained above is discredited, and also on the assumption that leadership is an individual activity, which we have been arguing against throughout this chapter. This should not be confused with appropriate uses of profiling to enable a person to understand more about their own strengths, weaknesses and predilections (Francis, 2014; Lamdin, 2012), and thus to understand more about what qualities they might wish to outsource to colleagues.

One of the stressors on people in the middle of any organization is the pressure to produce a number of different narratives to pass up and down the organization. There is the story that you tell your superior in order to keep him or her off your back and leave your congregation free to do what they need to be doing without worrying about the hierarchy. So you tell a story that shows all is well. Meanwhile you are also telling the congregation a story which suggests that the hierarchy are not as unhinged as at first appears, that their initiatives are capable of being usefully reinterpreted for the situation of your church, once again enabling them to get on with their mission and ministry. Then there is also the story that you tell to your fellow clergy about your dealings up and down the hierarchy. None of these stories will usually be false, but they contain variation, and the sheer number of them makes the whole enterprise hard work, and quite literally demoralizing. Anyone who needs to produce large numbers of stories to satisfy different audiences risks losing the plot of their own story (Sims, 2003).

Attempts at control can also leave people thoroughly bored with the distraction and effort of having to tell and retell their stories to people who do not really seem to be interested in the subtleties that make the difference. Appraisal systems often produce this effect for little gain. The last 20 years has seen the spread of regular reporting and form filling so that senior people can claim that they have stayed informed about what is happening on the ground. Neither the writers nor the readers of these reports gain from the experience, and it is yet another managerial fashion with no evidence at all to suggest that it has good effects. Also, the art of how to make your stories anodyne and safe may be one that is better not learned!

Stories and the love of small things

Leadership thinking is often very grandiose, very large scale, very important-sounding. Our final group of current elements in leadership discourse that we think particularly interesting for the Christian Church have to do with the importance of the less considered, smaller, apparently less significant people and actions.

> He has shown strength with his arm; he has scattered the proud in the thoughts of their hearts. He has brought down the powerful from their thrones, and lifted up the lowly; he has filled the hungry with good things, and sent the rich away empty. (Luke 1.51–53)

We noted in the previous chapter that the idea of servant leadership has been around as a counter to traditional hierarchical forms

for some time (Greenleaf, 1977). It has been taken up by investment banks and manufacturing companies, as well as churches
and synagogues. Its title says it all; leadership does not have to be
about being paid more, being able to give other people orders, and
being able to pass on undesirable tasks. Instead it can be about
serving those who are being led, and enabling them both to work
more effectively and to lead more fulfilling lives. Greenleaf is not
naïve, and does not suggest that tough decisions will not sometimes be needed. But even removing someone from a task which
they are not performing well and 'releasing' them for other activities can be a service, so long as it is sincerely and carefully done.
Block (1993) expresses a related idea:

> Stewardship . . . means giving people at the bottom and the
> boundaries of the organization choice over how to serve a cus-
> tomer, a citizen, a community. It is the willingness to be account-
> able for the well-being of the larger organization by operating
> in service, rather than in control, of those around us. Stated
> simply, it is accountability without control or compliance.

Related to this are ideas about authentic leadership (Goffee and
Jones, 2006; Ladkin and Spiller, 2013). 'Authenticity' has sometimes been used loosely, for example to imply that it is OK to do
anything so long as it feels right, because that must be authentic. Both of these books have gone well beyond that. Ladkin and
Spiller, for example, list several ways in which the contributors to
their book clash with earlier views of authentic leadership, many
of which are to do with the more recent understanding of authentic leading as a relational activity. Authenticity is seen in small
things. We judge authenticity from non-verbal cues, from details
of behaviour. Desmond Tutu tells the story of the impression
made on him as a small boy when his mother, a black cleaning
lady in apartheid South Africa, passed Fr Trevor Huddleston in
a corridor and the priest raised his hat respectfully and enquired
after her health. For Trevor Huddleston that was no doubt a very
small action, but it was seen as authentic by the small boy (and
children are expert judges of authenticity) and influenced him
profoundly.

Conant and Norgaard (2011) offer a similar thought. In what they describe as 'touchpoints' they say that leadership is not necessarily something that happens on a grand scale, but is part of every interaction, however trivial it might seem at the time. The minutiae of the coffee rota, making the arrangements for Messy Church, and talking to the musician who is upsetting the congregation are not distractions from the work of leadership; the way they are done is itself the act of leadership. Leadership is about genuine connection with others, and this requires the head (you know what you are trying to do), the heart (you have a genuine concern about the people you are working with) and the hands (you are competent, prepared, and you learn). It is implicit in this that if you value the touch points with others in your church, they are likely to mirror your way of being and also bring their heads, hearts and hands to co-operate with the leadership you are offering.

Much traditional management theory was based in a world of mechanism, where if you did A the consequence would be B, without any need for further discussion. As Harle (2012) has pointed out, this went with an understanding of the creation narrative in Genesis in which God is creating order out of chaos, and it goes with a Newtonian world view and a concern with control. Complexity theories, on the other hand, came initially from mathematics (Mandelbrot, 1982) and science, and are popularly associated with the idea that small changes can have big, remote impacts, sometimes referred to as the 'butterfly wings' effect. This is another way in which small things can become very important, another example of a leadership idea that might be particularly consonant with Christian faith:

> Then the righteous will answer him, 'Lord, when was it that we saw you hungry and gave you food, or thirsty and gave you something to drink? And when was it that we saw you a stranger and welcomed you, or naked and gave you clothing? And when was it that we saw you sick or in prison and visited you?' And the king will answer them, 'Truly I tell you, just as you did it to one of the least of these who are members of my family, you did it to me.' (Matthew 25.37–40)

Organizations excel when someone loves them into life (Sims, 2004). This can be observed in schools, churches, hospitals, banks or almost anywhere. If an organization appears to be punching above its weight, you can usually find people who behave to it in a more loving way than they have to. A narrative view of love is that, when people are willing to intertwine their stories with one another's, or with those of a church or other organization, this is love (Sims, 2004). Leadership often fails to value such loving attention, and does serious damage to the love that some church members wish to pour into their church. We suggested above that the stories that are effective in leading people are the ones they can get involved with, the ones where they can find a role and character for themselves so that they become part of the story (Roberts, 2014). This is strengthened if they can find a way so that their own story and that of their church are intertwined. Long-term relationships between people are those where each party has decided that the other's story will become part of their own. This also becomes a loving relationship where both parties are prepared to encourage the other's story to intertwine with their own. Leaders in churches who would like members to love the church will have to be prepared for a few tendrils to wind themselves around unexpected places. Love is not easily controlled.

Others have pointed out that charismatic leaders are always talked about in a way that is very similar to love. We will come back to charismatic leadership, and why we think it can be dangerous, but it is worth noting here that charisma works by having others fall in love with you (Denning, 2008). This works in reverse, too. For example, we can see in the popular reaction to political leaders that they are often accepted or rejected in terms that are more reminiscent of physical attraction or repulsion, rather than on the basis of what they actually do or say. We either identify with them, or we may shudder at everything they say, but it is more like an aesthetic judgement than an intellectual one. Accepting another's leadership can be like a love story, which is one of the motivations to lead.

We noted in Chapter 1 that Ladkin (2008) has written about the notion of 'leading beautifully', suggesting that we have a lot more to understand about leadership when we look beyond what is done to how it is done. She suggests that mastery, congruence and purpose are all aspects that we read in a leadership performance, and influence how we take it; this brings us back to Conant and Norgaard's (2011) head, heart and hands. Leading beautifully also connects with paying attention to small things; the precise wording of a prayer, crafting of a sermon or phrasing of an announcement are all areas in which leadership can be loving. Grisham (2006) has pointed out that cadence, metre and rhyme are part of how we hear a story. Stories are not only selected sequences of events, but are told with more or less linguistic power. The good story has an aesthetic presentation that is important to its power. Gharibyan-Kefalloniti and Sims (2012) quote a merchant marine captain who told them that, on board ship at times of tension, using the wrong word could be more dangerous than a loaded gun. Choosing the right word was, for this captain, a loving form of leadership on his ship.

Conclusion: Stories and the Good News

The church is a storytelling organization. It has a story to tell to those inside and outside, a story that it values and that it believes is well worth telling. The Gospels frequently present Jesus as a story-teller, and many of the most loved passages of the Bible are stories. Storytelling is a sacred activity in the Christian faith. Leadership within the Church is principally the leadership of storytelling, and it can be conducted through storytelling. Perhaps we need to recover a sense that we all are, or should be, storytellers, and that we need to lead and be led in a way that develops that storytelling capacity and makes us more effective storytellers, as well as making our lives better stories. Only then will we be ready to join in with giving a (storied) account of the hope that is in us.

Questions

1 Think of the narratives that have been important in your understanding of the Church. Are they biblical, historical, theological,
   personal, other stories or a mixture?

2 What has been your experience of leaders using stories in their leadership roles? Has this been healthy and affirming or an attempt to exert undue power and control? Can you think of examples of good 'storied' leadership?

3 Reflecting upon your encounters in church life and practice, can you think of times when attention to small details or touch points would have affected a church's story for the better?

3

Stories and Identities:
Story, Character and Becoming

We live in and by stories. The way we see ourselves influences, or determines, the stories we choose to join and the characters we develop for ourselves in those stories. We will choose to see and live by particular kinds of story that fit with how we see ourselves. Part of making that choice and then feeling fully involved in the story is that we forget that we ever made a choice or that we had actually crafted a story; our story is our story, and we are too busy living inside it to think of it as something we chose or created.

This chapter starts by looking at some of the well-known ways of telling stories and the consequences that our choice of how to tell a story has for the effectiveness of ourselves and our organizations. It goes on to talk about some ways of telling stories which may make it hard – perhaps unnecessarily hard – for the organization to work well and positively, and then to types of plot which can be built into stories and which have consequences for the potential actions that present themselves to the inhabitants of these stories. It discusses the idea that people follow stories rather than leaders, and then some issues of who finds themselves able, and who not able, to tell stories. After a section on why we cannot reduce stories to simple propositions and structures, we go on to discuss the stories that really fly and that support identity best.

Giants and grasshoppers

Beaumont (2010) retells the story of the spies who were sent by Moses into the land of Canaan to assess the challenges of invading the land. They came back with a frightening report, that while the land was rich ('flowing with milk and honey'), the people of the land were like giants beside whom the people of Israel were like grasshoppers. Famously, there was also a minority report from Joshua the son of Nun and Caleb the son of Jephunneh with a much more optimistic view of the prospects. Numbers 13 tells of how these two competing story lines played out. Beaumont regards the majority report of the spies as a typical reaction to anxiety on the part of congregational storytellers. People are stuck in a version of the story which can in some ways be comforting, because it is so familiar; we are doing our best, but our situation is fundamentally hopeless.

But why should that be comforting? We can become accustomed to telling particular kinds of story about ourselves, and our identity fits easily with the characters we take on in those stories. There are not many who would claim, if asked, that they enjoy failing or that they wish to fail, but there are many who are so accustomed to telling stories of their own failure that this is the most comfortable place for them to be. They have rehearsed stories of failure at length, have learned to tell them well, perhaps wittily and certainly with an endearing degree of self-deprecation. They have learned how to make a good story out of failure. Peers says of one minister:

> Her tendency to be the rescuer and save the day when others didn't follow through made her the hero in her tragic story about them – and about her. When she recognized that her hero or rescuer role was part of her tragic story, she realized she was part of the problem. (Peers, 2010, pp. 46–7)

In this case awareness of the story that she had got stuck in was all the minister needed to start embodying and living a different story. She did not need to see herself as alone and courageous; others were with her if she relaxed the story enough to be able to see them. A similar changing of a story to produce a change in the way somebody sees what is going on appears in 1 Kings 19.18, where Elijah is challenged by God on the heroic role he is scripting for himself in a tragic story. The heroism of the lonely Christian fighting the forces of darkness (typified by tales such as Bunyan's *Pilgrim's Progress*) may sometimes be one of the possible accurate ways of telling the story, but it has narrative attractions which should make us question whether it is the most effective way of understanding what is going on. Geoff Mead (2017) suggests that stories in which we cast ourselves as heroes are only really satisfying at a fairly early life stage; and Heriot (2016) suggests that stories in which we are cast as heroes in a battle are especially attractive to some Christian groups, who are only happy if they can show that they have a fight on their hands. That fight might be motivated more by the desire to create a good narrative than by anybody actually benefiting from the fight.

This is related to the need that many of us have for problems. Problems can be stressful, time consuming, confidence sapping and so on, but do we want to be without them? To solve someone else's problem can amount to theft. It was theirs. It was part of who they are, their identity. They may have suffered for it – in which case they are likely to be all the more committed to it. Parry (2008) says that 'organizational stories seem to have a general theme about overcoming adversity' (p. 133). For some people, to live a fully storied life, the adversity is necessary; otherwise the story is not exciting enough for them to care about.

Shapiro (2010) suggests that congregations live by one or more sacred stories. One or two stories from the Bible particularly appeal to that congregation, and are used to describe the core of what their life is about. He gives the example of a particularly hospitable congregation who will relish the story of Abraham and Sarah welcoming the visitors who foretold the birth of Isaac. Where such stories operate, they are like a connecting root system, throwing up shoots all over the place which turn out to be outgrowths of the same plant.

One of us was involved in a church that had a sacred story about what could and could not be done given that the majority of its local population was Muslim. Not many churches in the UK will claim the adherence of most of their local population, so the fact that many of the local population, whether or not they are adherents of another faith, were even less likely than usual to be recruited to the life of the church might be seen as not making much difference. But again and again stories were told about what this church could not try as part of its mission and outreach because of the predominance of another faith in its local population.

Stories that enshrine the negative

If stories are chosen and crafted by the people who tell them, and sometimes by those who inhabit them, can we give any guidance as to what ways of crafting a story may be most helpful in terms of likely outcomes?

On September 11, 2001, planes were crashed into each of the twin towers of the World Trade Center in New York, killing 2,977 people. The television pictures were horrific, and there was a public feeling of terror that people could be murdered so quickly, in such large numbers, with so little warning, in a safe part of the world, while going about their mundane duties in offices in tall buildings. The President of the United States was under pressure to come up very quickly with a story to describe what had happened, and what America's actions would be in response to what had happened. The phrase that George W. Bush came up with on 20 September was 'the war on terror'. America was at war, it had been attacked by terrorists, and the response was to be an attack on terror itself. Sympathy for the United States was widespread in the western world, and other countries, including the UK, promised to give whatever support they could to America's war on terror. The wars in Afghanistan and Iraq followed as part of this war on terror.

The situation immediately after the attack on the twin towers was confused and felt desperate; there was a longing to find a story to understand what was going on and a story within which to act. Looking back, in a world where the long-term consequences of that war have been destabilization of the Middle East and the threat of much more terror and destruction, it does not look like a very good way of telling the story, because:

1 Terror is an abstraction, and it does not make much sense to fight a war against an abstraction.

2 Most of the perpetrators of the attacks on the World Trade Center, and most of the funding, came from Saudi Arabia, which was never targeted in the war on terror.

3 The movement of currency and commodity markets in the days before the attacks suggested that some investors knew there was about to be a calamity, and were positioning themselves to make money out of it.

So the story could have been told as a massive financial crime, involving the murder of thousands of people in order to make a profit. If the story had been told that way, we might have been saved several wars, the displacement of hundreds of thousands or possibly millions of refugees, and dangerous tensions within and around the Middle East. The way a story is told has real consequences.

Bass (2010) points out that church stories are often told as if they were a version of the story of the *Titanic*. We are heading for the iceberg, are about to have a catastrophic crash, and most of us will be killed. This is indeed just how some in the Church of England are telling its story currently, emphasizing that it is 'one generation away from extinction'. Of course no organization is ever more than one generation from extinction, but this way of telling the story creates a good heroic character for those who would like to be seen as riding to the rescue. But, Bass says, what if the story told is that of the *Mayflower*, not the *Titanic*?

> In the *Titanic* story, leaders lead while the ship is sinking. In the *Mayflower* story, leadership stabilizes a Pilgrim community in choppy seas as they head for an unknown world. Leadership in a crisis? Or leadership as an adventure? How a leader leads and the expectations a community has about leadership depends on the stories we tell ourselves. (Bass, 2010, pp. 153–4)

Stories shape leaders as much as leaders shape stories. People tell stories that show themselves in a good light. You occasionally find groups who will tell stories about how their own failings have driven the downward path of their church, but much more commonly a story is told that demonizes somebody, often the minister, and sometimes some denominational body which is beyond the control of the local church. In everyday life in organizations we can never be completely sure what is causing what, which means that the choices that everyone is left with as to how to attribute blame or success are very open. You will very rarely hear, 'We are growing, and nobody knows why.' You are much more likely to hear a story that hypothesizes the reasons for what is going on, but in reality this is guesswork. But it is guesswork which has real consequences for the health and future of the organization concerned, and which is often heavily influenced by either the political interests or the habits of thought of the storytellers. If you think that either the growth or the decline of your local church can be explained by the approach it takes to the Bible, you are likely, without any intent to distort the truth, to tell stories that illustrate this.

The plot thickens

The Canadian literary critic C. Northrop Frye (1957) proposed four narrative archetypes or plots, and suggested that most of our storytelling followed these archetypes (for a fuller description, see NeoEnglish, 2010). Put very briefly, Frye suggests that some stories may be developed with a tragic plot, in which circumstances are so great in opposition to the hero of the story that we can see that everything is bound to go wrong from the outset. The hero of the tragic plot has free will; they do not have to undergo the torments and suffering that the story brings them, but they do so even though we and possibly they can see that they will not succeed. Other stories have a comic plot, in which the action takes place against a background of chance events, which seem to have no concern for, or relation with, the desires and intentions of the main actors. The characters are rarely presented as heroes and are not in control of events, which nevertheless turn out well. Others have a romantic plot, where the virtuous and righteous hero will conquer enormous odds and opposition to win through, often against a demonic enemy. Finally, there are ironic or satirical plots, with a sense of the absurd and improbable. Nothing makes much sense, and events do not turn out as you would wish. Ironic plots are like romantic plots gone wrong, where things do not mysteriously fall into place. NeoEnglish gives David and Goliath as an example of an ironic plot, where the little person improbably overcomes the greater person, though this could also be thought of as a romantic plot. Ironic for Goliath, romantic for David, perhaps.

As with many features of storied living, people are often unaware of the choices they are making about the plots in which they tell themselves as stories. We rehearse how to live out particular kinds of plot, how to make meaning of our lives within them. Although the tragic plot with its inevitable ultimate failure may not sound attractive, if that is the kind of plot that you are used to living in, there is an incentive to cast the events in front of you into another tragic plot. You know who you are when you are the doomed, tragic hero. You know how to present yourself to yourself and others. You may not like the outcome, but you are well practised in how to cope with it and admire yourself in it. We know a family of siblings, all of whom have had difficult and frustrating lives, all of whom blame their parents. Such a way of telling their story does not lead to any change. Their parents are dead, and the siblings are all grown up. From an outside perspective, their diagnosis of their problem is not necessarily inaccurate. Their parents were strange and rather distant, but as a way of telling their story, this is a disabling plot to use. They might well be happier and more effective if they could find a way of recasting the story, perhaps as a comedy. There are plenty of churches with a similarly unproductive way of telling their story. Maybe they are still coping with problems arising from poor decisions by previous members and leaders, but they cannot change the past, so this is not going to lead to effective action. They could, of course, rewrite their past as a more productive story, enabling them to give themselves a more positive future – but then they would lose the comforting joy of telling well-rehearsed stories to blame others.

Many organizations are seen ironically by their members. The signs around offices saying, 'You don't have to be mad to work here, but it helps' are an ironic emplotment. Many churches talk about their central denominational organizations in ironic terms; regulations, suggestions, mission statements and ways of measuring

effectiveness come pouring out of regional or national-level organizations, and are received locally with a shrug, or with resentment
at yet another activity that takes active people away from what
they think should be their priorities. The local leadership may try
to retell the story as a comedy: 'This is what they are asking of us
centrally, isn't that funny? But it doesn't really matter.' Thus the
local leadership tries to preserve the activity and engagement levels
of church members by holding an umbrella over them to protect
them from the demands of the national church.

You will have your own preferences for particular plots, as will
those you work with in your local church. The practical value of
understanding Frye's plots is that, if you know how you usually
emplot the circumstances around you, the awareness may give
you more choice about how you emplot situations in future. Are
you happy with the proportion of tragedies, comedies, ironies
or romances that you see? One bishop we talked to became very
angry at the idea that he was choosing to see the church through
tragic plots. He believed that he saw it that way because that was
reality. This is exactly our point. We construct reality in certain
ways, tell certain types of story, and come to believe that this is
objectively how they are. The possibility of reconstructing the plot
gives us more choice about how we make things better.

Following stories

As we said in Chapter 2, Parry (2008) makes the argument that
'people follow organizational stories as much as they follow people,
so organizational stories can be considered as leadership' (p. 127).
We commonly tell stories about people. We expect a story to have
a hero, or a central character, and probably some other characters
around them. We are suspicious of accounts of things happening without there being a person involved in their happening –
although this does not seem to make us as suspicious as we should
be of potentially meaningless phrases such as 'the goals of the
organization' or 'the will of the people'. However, as Parry points
out, it seems that people sometimes join in the narrative more than

they follow the leader. The story is not just a vehicle for leadership; it is what leads. Followership occurs because people identify themselves as a character in the story and start living in it. They base their actions within the story. At some stage someone crafted the story and put it into circulation, but the story is now doing the leading.

Parry goes on to argue that 'we embed ourselves in stories until we find the story that makes sense' (p. 132). In other words, we keep experimenting with stories, trying them on, to see which one fits our sense of ourselves, and gives us outcomes that we like. Sixty years of leadership research have not even produced an agreed definition, he points out. All that we can usefully discuss is what works for people, and his research suggests that the notion of finding a story that works for you and joining in with it is a good description of how leadership works that resonates for many within organizations. It is interestingly close to the phrase that we quoted in Chapter 2 that Christian mission is 'finding out what God is doing, and joining in'. Training and development in leadership for churches would be focused rather differently as a result.

This only works if stories are taken really seriously. Not everyone who talks about the importance of story is above making some rather dubious, instrumental uses of story to influence others in the direction demanded by their own interests and preoccupations. A story can be told in a heavily slanted way that makes clear what listeners are supposed to do when they hear it. One of us heard the following story told in a sermon in our childhood.

A man and his small son were walking home in the middle of the day, and they were passing the church clock. 'Boing' went the clock, and the little boy looked up and smiled, because he liked the sound, and said 'One'. 'Boing' went the clock again, 'Two' said the boy, and so on up to twelve. But then the clock struck a thirteenth time, and the little boy looked up at his father and said, 'Daddy, it's never been this late before.'

The point of this story was to give a particular view about the second coming of Jesus, and to show the urgency of commitment to Christ for the listeners and their friends. The story was effective in that we still remember it from almost a lifetime ago. But it was making such a specific point, and its interpretation was so much built into the story, that it did not engage the imagination as much as a less controlling story would have done. It scores well on memorability, but not on influence. A story that left the interpretation more in the hands of the listeners might have been more influential. As Keel (2007) puts it:

> Unfortunately, rather than living deeply within scriptural stories in a way that shapes our imagination, we use them in a way that kills it. We reduce these stories to prescriptions for how churches in all times ought to respond regardless of context. (p. 168)

He suggests that we rely on systems of control and structures of belief to take the hard work and dependence on the Holy Spirit out of our response to stories, and thus greatly weaken their impact on us. The way stories, including scriptural stories, impact on people is beyond our control, a theme we shall return to. Keel describes this process thus:

> The Bible becomes a natural resource to be strip-mined for precious and pure ores of theological truth. While we may enjoy possessing and looking at such shiny nuggets of theological wealth, when we go back to the Bible we discover that we have devastated the original resource, which once possessed a natural, magnificent and even terrifying beauty. (pp. 170–1)

Being able to tell stories

Henry James said that stories happen to people who are able to tell them, by which he meant that the raw occurrence of events only becomes a story when a person makes it into one. Stories only become stories when they are constructed by people. Can everyone tell stories? We cannot think of anyone who can't, but storytelling ability and style clearly vary considerably. If we think back to the claim in Chapter 2 that we remember by narrative, as well as by living, dreaming, and so on, it is hard to imagine a person not being able to engage in storytelling. There is simply too much around us, too many events, too much environment, for us to be able to tell anybody everything, so what we tell will always be a selective story, and anyone who could not tell such a story would lead a very difficult life. We select according to our audience, according to our purpose in telling, and according to the story in which we see ourselves.

We are marinated in stories. They come at us from all forms of media as well as from the people we interact with. All this experience with stories gives us the basis for our storytelling skill. We see somebody else tell a story, and we see its effect on others. As we are listening to their story we may be considering which story of our own we wish to use in response to what we are hearing. Or we may be thinking about whether the person telling the story is casting themselves in the light they would choose, and whether they will be happy with the reception of their story by others. If you are telling your minister a story and they are looking over your shoulder while you are telling it, you understand the feedback quickly. Your story was not catching the attention. We edit our stories according to what we know goes down well with the audience. One of us had a boss who wanted numbers for everything. It took us a while to realize that the bits of our story that he was listening to were completely different from the bits of our story that we thought were most important. We were skipping over the quantified parts of our story, and he was skipping over the qualitative parts. He was the boss, so we had to learn. In order to learn, we had to listen to parts of others' stories for which we might previously have switched off. Listening to others' stories is a way of increasing our own repertoire and range of storytelling skill.

There is some debate in training ministers as to how personal the stories should be that are told. There is a fear that stories may be self-indulgent, that people may end up disclosing for the sake of doing so. Against this, Anderson (2010) relates how he told a painful, personal and current story to his congregation, and found this a rewarding and releasing experience. 'I released my anxious pain into the hands of the congregation. I watched in amazement as their hands were miraculously transformed into Christ's hands' (p. 114). He goes on to talk about how ministerial formation can often lead to ministers feeling much more comfortable listening to stories rather than telling their own. But when he took the risk of telling a difficult and personal story to his congregation, his experience was that they 'grabbed my story lines and wove them into their own'. This is what happens with stories. Someone tells a story and we relate to it as it reminds us of parts of our story, which we may see differently and become able to work with when we hear this other story. Sometimes we will then want to write ourselves into their story, but more often their story line enriches our understanding of our own story. Of course, it means being prepared to override the pressure on both ministers and members of the congregation to have others believe that you are perfect!

The downside of this is that, if we are open in the stories we tell, and then listen to the stories that others tell back, we may fear the potential avalanche of stories; will we ever get away and be able to get on with the rest of our work? One of us was involved in a research project where we were publicly noting on a flipchart the points made by members of a meeting. An unexpected consequence of this was that members of the meeting repeated themselves far less, and reports from some members said that this was especially the case with those who were notorious for repetition. We concluded that people repeat themselves because they do not think they have been heard. When people know they have been heard they are more likely to avoid repetition, and sometimes even to be more selective about what stories they tell. The avalanche is self-correcting.

Stories do not reduce to propositions

There is a risk in our discussion of effectiveness in storytelling and story listening that we start thinking too instrumentally, as if stories were just a clever means for enabling people to convey propositions to one another. We can lose sight of the holistic and mysterious nature of stories. A lot of social research mines stories for the ideas that are conveyed in the story. This extractive process, the finding of nuggets in the slush, does not do justice to the way that people live in and through stories. One of the special things about stories is that they can hold several different events or ideas together. A story always has some redundancy in it, some lines that are not necessary to the overall burden of the narrative. Good stories will include some points that, when you hear them, you simply do not know whether they are essential to the story. Stories carry some inefficiency. They could be trimmed, but trim them too far and they die. 'King Uzziah died' is not a story, but a statement of fact. 'In the year that King Uzziah died'(Isaiah 6.1) is still not a story, but it references a story, which you can then go and find elsewhere. Analysing stories for their most important facts is tempting, but it can easily lead to missing the point, which is only to be found in the holistic character of the story, and often only to be found in the interaction between the listener and that holistic character. Keel (2007) talks about the stories that visitors to his church look for:

> They then seek to discover what is unique in our environment that they can export to their churches in order to *reproduce* whatever particular manifestation of life they see in our community and long for in theirs. Such efforts are doomed to failure. (p. 215)

> We are often not able to read stories and allow them to ignite our local imaginations. Instead we try to mine stories for timeless principles that can be readily applied. (p. 80)

Because stories take time to hear and to appreciate, and because we all feel under pressure to be getting on to the next thing, the pressure is always with us to reduce stories to their bare bones, or to a summarized plot line. It doesn't work. It no longer functions as a story. Sometimes, too, those who are trying to lead in churches feel they have run out of story; they simply do not know where to take the story next, which is the leadership equivalent of writer's block.

The 'best' stories

What makes for a really 'good' story, and what makes a story weak? 'Good' is obviously a difficult word here; is a story that is convincing and entertaining but that leads people into self-destructive behaviour good? Is it possible to have a good story badly told, or a poor story well performed? This chapter is about stories and identities; is a good story one that fits well with your identity, or that helps you to express or to develop your identity?

Denning (2001) introduced the idea of springboard stories, those that enable action to take off in hitherto impossible directions. He summarizes the idea in Denning, 2011a, as follows:

A springboard story is a story that describes an example in which the change idea that the speaker is proposing has already happened, at least in part. If a leader can find such a story and the story resonates with listeners, it can connect with them at an emotional level and generate a new story in their minds in a way that leads to action. However, because a springboard story is positive in tone, it may be less effective initially in getting the listeners' attention than a question or a story about the listeners' own problems! (p. 160)

The idea of resonance in this quotation is quite widespread in the literature on leadership by storytelling. The quality of a good story is that it strikes a note that sets something off in its listeners, that they find themselves caught by. This is quite separate from whether it is true, or whether it is aesthetically pleasing. Denning argues that our attention is more likely to be caught by a negative story ('the church is declining'), but that such stories produce no action, whereas a positive story ('here are the green shoots of growth') is more likely to go unnoticed but, if it is heard, is more likely to be a springboard to action.

Rendle (2010) argues that narrative leaders need to move people 'beyond fears to hope, beyond remembered pasts to present and future potential, beyond limited resources to unbounded possibility' (pp. 27–8). This is not easy. We have an enormous capacity to live long in a weak story, for example a nostalgic story of how the church used to be full of young people every Sunday and had a huge programme of exciting activities. Such weak stories are safe ones for a congregation to retreat to, because they do not imply any action – it is all beyond their control, and is the fault of someone else, or demographics, or the times. A community that harbours such stories may be quite happy in the process of declining together. Rendle suggests that the important thing in leading in this situation is to say, 'You're better than that.' He quotes Howard Gardner's suggestion that the central task of leadership is to give people a better story to live. Not necessarily more convincing, not necessarily one that they enjoy more, but one that is a springboard to a better future.

Some stories have stronger structures than others. Writing for film makers, McKee (1999) says:

> Structure is a selection of events from the characters' life stories that is composed into a strategic sequence to arouse specific emotions and to express a specific view of life. (p. 33)

Stories should have just enough fat on them. Strip them of all redundancies and irrelevancies and they become flat and unconvincing, more like a series of statements without the stardust that makes a story. Allow too great a profusion of different ideas and strands in the story and they lose focus; your listeners become unsure what the story is about, or what the main line through the story is supposed to be. A story that gives the listener no choice of how to interpret it will not capture the imagination, because being caught by a story is always the result of our own active response to it.

The stories of a community need to be coherent but not necessarily consistent. Linde (1993) suggests that life stories can be coherent only if they are to some extent inconsistent. She gives the example of how she came to be a social anthropologist working for NASA. She has several different ways she can tell the story, but has to be careful not to tell more than one of them to the same audience because they appear to be mutually conflicting. One is a romantic story about how she had always felt that she should put her social anthropology to wider use, and eventually found this opportunity. Another is a comic story about how she happened to be seen on local television one night by the Head of NASA, talking about something different but related, and her employment at NASA stemmed from this chance event, and so on. We expect stories to grow and change as they go along, which in the literature is referred to as 'narrative arc'. If a story develops in a straight line it is neither credible nor interesting; arcs give life.

Standish (2010) suggests that there must be some consonance between a congregation's story and its pastoral leader's story if we are to avoid confusion. We suspect that there are many more than simply these two stories that need to be reconciled. There are the congregations for different services (for example, the chronically different story of those who attend 8.00 a.m. services in the Church of England), there are different interest groups and people whose stories are spinning in different directions. The task for those leading is to hear these different stories without getting so caught up in any one of them that they ignore the others. Then it is to build collaboration between the different groups to form a story that all can work with. This seems to happen best not by setting up story-telling sessions, but by getting members of the groups that sustain the different stories working on projects together. Immediately, people find themselves living together in the same story, and this builds the love and understanding within which new stories can be nurtured.

Questions

1 Think of a time when you have seen a church with a story that enshrines the negative. What was done, or what could have been done, to change the storytelling to something more helpful for the future, more *Mayflower*, less *Titanic*?

2 Are there people in your church who are not encouraged to tell their stories? If so, does this matter?

3 Think of two examples of springboard stories that you have seen at work in churches. If it was difficult to think of them, why do you think this was the case?

4

Living in Multiple Stories

A way of seeing is always a way of not seeing, and viewing life as storied also has its limitations. There is an important difference between our life experience as people and the way that many stories work. We live simultaneously in many different stories. A character in a play or a novel lives in one main story with perhaps some references to other stories of which they are a part, and which may bring extra complexity to the main story line. For example, the hero of a detective story is cleverly and bravely gathering information and making sense of it, while also coping with the decline of an elderly parent and dealing with the aftermath of a failed love affair. There are three stories going on here, but one of them is the main story, with the others as subsidiaries. As readers, we usually have the author's help to stay with the main story; as people, we are making continuous choices about which of our stories are main and which are subsidiary.

In churches, church life will figure in a different way for different people in the story, and they will also have expectations about how it should figure for others. Congregations will expect that the story of their church is important to their minister, and they may well also take more seriously other members of the congregation for whom the church seems to be a major part of their story. This can, of course, lead to a very inward-looking group of people, who only take seriously others who are as fascinated by the church as they are themselves. Lest we think this is just a church problem, the same thing can happen, in many organizations, to marketing people whose work and focus is outside the organization. Others may see that this is essential for the health of their company, but still be slightly suspicious of the amount of time and focus that marketers give to the outside, and upset if they see such people being promoted. They are 'sleeping with the enemy'.

This chapter is about some of the effects that these multiple stories can have on church life. We start from the locus of stories; stories can be told about a denomination, a building, a congregation or the gospel. We move on to look at stories and time, where stories can be told about the past, the present or the future. Within each of these divisions there can be different orientations; what is foregrounded as important within this story? Is it about purity, or evangelism, or about the effect of the church on the wider world? Stories are told within tribes, and in ways that appeal to other members of the tribe, which means that some of the multiple stories that are available to be told will not be visible to members of some tribes, while being seen as self-evidently the only way of seeing the world by members of other tribes. This takes us on to a consideration of the relationship between stories and truth. Stories are not inherently more or less truthful than any other way of speaking. People tell the truth through stories, just as they might through a set of statistics, and they may also use either form of communication to mislead other people. The relationship between stories and trust is also very important, and there is quite a lot that needs to be said about the mutual trust that is required among a community for people to allow each other to become authors of stories. Finally, we shall offer a typology from Gabriel (2016) that we find helpful for thinking about the ecology of stories.

The locus of stories

Within a church, there are a number of different ways that stories can be located. First, there is the gospel story. This may at first not appear particularly prominent, but most churches have particular ways of telling it. For example, a Christmas carol service is usually designed to tell the story of the incarnation, a service on Easter Eve may be designed to tell the story of salvation, and the Eucharist is designed to tell the story of the Last Supper. The stories are often told with physical layout as well as words. Church reordering is often done to tell a story more effectively. The prominence of the pulpit or the altar in different churches can tell you something about the prevalence of different stories in that particular church, and if the layout does not fit with the story the church wants to tell there will be pressure to reorder it. Small details of how the story of faith is told come to assume great importance. In some churches it is very important that the bread for the Eucharist comes from a single loaf, and that the loaf should be as ordinary as possible. In other churches the importance of relating the story to Jesus' last Passover supper is key, so they see it as equally important that the bread should not be leavened. There is no unanimity about which parts of the gospel story must be told, or in what order, or with what degrees of emphasis for their importance.

Church buildings often symbolize the stories being told, and the story of the building itself is often valued highly. Some congregations are keen to tell you the story of their building. One of us recently visited a church where friendly members of the congregation took us straight out at the end of the service to show us their baptistery, which had recently been beautified, and which they obviously regarded as the part of their church most worth looking at. Church buildings often tell a story of faith with different emphases from the current day. Old wall paintings may tell Bible stories for an illiterate congregation, sometimes with degrees of violence that seem positively pornographic today. High ceilings may emphasize the eminence rather than the immanence of God, and the place where children worship always tells its own story. As do notice boards and websites, which are often the quickest way for a visitor to know if this is a church where they would like to develop their own story.

The relationship between a church building and the church's story is not necessarily seen as positive. Many ministers and lay leaders see their church buildings as a weight around their necks. They are trying to proclaim the gospel story afresh to a new generation, while the building seems to them to symbolize all the wrong things. The building may seem to suggest that the church is wealthy, powerful and awe-inspiring when they want to say that the church is poor, serving and inclusive. Old church buildings can often absorb inordinate amounts of time and money which the church would like to be devoting to the current needs of those around it. Many older buildings were built in the expectation of growth, and were never full, exacerbating the story of decline that a sparse congregation tells. Sometimes the stories can be about fittings rather than the whole building; we have a beautiful new red carpet, which we certainly should not put at risk by allowing people to eat food near it. Or, these pews were good enough for previous generations and should not be replaced, however uncomfortable modern softies might find them.

The congregation's story is different again, though often connected with the building's story. The congregation can often tell you about important characters from their past, who in some cases are seen as heroic defenders of all the congregation stands for. Quite a few churches have stories about when they fell on hard times, but the determination of one or two faithful members refused to accept defeat, and times became better. Some of these stories are about how the congregation came into being, which may be a story of a church plant, or of a denomination realizing that it was not represented in a particular area, or of an individual with a vision of what a church might do in a particular place. Founder myths like these are common in many kinds of organization. There are major companies that do not serve alcohol in their residential training establishments because their (long dead) founders would not have approved. Sometimes these stories are now regarded with some humour because the context in which they arose is so different. One congregation and building that we knew was founded for fear that the poor might be seduced to a different denomination whose nearby church had more seating available. This story was told with a smile in an era when shortage of seating was a problem that the congregation (and others around it) could only dream of.

Even in these more ecumenical days there is also a denominational story. Often the theological differences that split churches in the past are not so salient in the present, but most churches have a number of occasions on which they tell their denominational story, and remind themselves as to why they are different from others. This could be a dedication festival, a covenant service, or an annual set of special meetings. Others may not see the distinctive contribution of another denomination as having that much current importance, but if you say so to a member, you may get a response such as 'We might not be so concerned about this now, but all the same, people died for this belief.' Often the denominational stories give you the background as to why some difference that seems tiny to non-members is important. This is reminiscent of Freud's notion of 'the narcissism of small differences', whereby differences that are almost undetectable to outsiders assume enormous importance to those who are on either side of that difference (Freud, 2015).

Stories and time

Stories connect time in a distinctive way. Stories can be told about the past, the present or the future. Stories about one time period have implications for other time periods, but remain focused on their own period. For example, a church leader can articulate a story about how the church will engage in a particular type of mission. This story may be told so as to suggest continuity (it's what our founder, or the late Mrs Goggins, or whoever, would have wanted) or to suggest something new (we have never really engaged with that housing estate).

Sometimes a story will be told with a back story which is supposed to explain where the church is now ('another church was needed that could be attended by the servants of the people who attended the main church, and then another one specifically for the quarry workers, whose boots might have damaged the floor'), but Cannadine (1983) has shown that quite often traditions are invented to support what is being done now. The suggestion that the British coronation ceremony can be traced back to the coronation of King Edgar the Peaceable in Bath Abbey in 973 came in a television commentary, whereas closer examination suggests that very little of it can be traced earlier than the twentieth century. But the story persisted, and demonstrates the power with which a back story can be developed to support a later tradition.

The tendency for stories to occupy different time zones is often used as an act of aggression against someone else's story. Those who tell stories of the past know that the past is the only time when we can claim to know what happened, but they are belittled as backward looking or 'living in the past' by those who tell stories of the future or the present. Those who tell stories of the future, of how things might be, have to cope with sometimes being dismissed as dreamers. Those who tell stories of the present may see themselves as the most grounded and real of all storytellers, but they are open to attack from different interpretations of what is happening in the present, in which almost everyone sees themselves as an expert. Mather (2010) talks about making sure that stories about the past, present and future are all honoured in a church:

> Once a month in worship, right before the final hymn, we celebrate ministries that have died, ministries that are continuing, and ministries that are beginning. (p. 139)

By celebrating stories of the past, present and future they recognize faithful service in the past and present alongside the excitement of the future, and honour all of these. This takes care of a problem for many organizations, that stories about the past tend to become stories either about a supposed golden age, or about 'bad old days', 'before we saw the light', and those most involved are either canonized or devalued, both equally destructive. It is one of the areas in which the curation of stories, which we shall discuss more in Chapter 5, becomes very important.

Parry and Hansen (2007) say that 'every future-focused story is a proposal for action, detailing what behaviours lead to various ends, and how' (p. 286). Telling future stories has been undervalued in organizational life. Families do it when considering the holidays they are going to have, but to do it at work risks looking silly when the future does not come to plan. As Bennis said (1970): 'The future is a conscious dream, a set of imaginative hypotheses groping toward whatever vivid utopias lie at the heart of our consciousness.' This is close to the imagery of Martin Luther King, and suggests that future storytelling might be very powerful.

As we saw in Chapter 3, Keel (2007) speaks of one of the ways in which we miss the excitement of future storytelling: 'Unfortunately, rather than living deeply within scriptural stories in a way that shapes our imagination, we use them in a way that kills it' (p. 168). He then quotes Hauerwas and Willimon (1989), who say: 'In Jesus we meet not a presentation of basic ideas about God, world, and humanity, but an invitation to join up, to become part of the movement, a people' (p. 21). Future stories invite us to join, to be led by the story, reminding us of the quotation from Parry that we used in Chapter 3, that leadership is done by stories rather than by people.

The orientation of stories

What kinds of story are current or can reasonably easily be told in any particular church? Roozen, McKinney and Carroll (1984) suggest four different orientations, which are not mutually exclusive and which are likely to influence the predominance of particular kinds of story in a church. There is a sanctuary orientation, where the church sees itself as providing a safe place for people to shelter from the storms of life. There is an evangelistic orientation, where the church sees itself as mainly there to win new converts. There is a civic orientation, where the church is there to serve others and to make things better for everyone; and there is an activist orientation, where the church takes its responsibility as being to change society in what it sees as a more healthy and fulfilling direction. Within the cultures of these churches there will of course be some members who wish to live out one of the other orientations and to move the church's story in that direction, but such stories will not be easily received, and are likely to become hard work for the tellers. It is not difficult to disaffirm a storyteller whose orientation you do not like. We are all quite skilled at withholding the cues that imply approval of what is being said.

Keel (2007) suggests that all these orientations may be declining, because he sees the world as subject to increasing fragmentation, balkanization and atomization. Big structures do not express the needs and aspirations of the twenty-first century.

We do not need more Christian leaders building church empires at a time when our culture is dismantling other such structures around us. We must deconstruct ourselves in love. (p. 111)

The days of powerfully unified churches with a common orientation are past, in this view. Now, worshippers will want to be allowed 'to discover a future together under God' (p. 112) instead of being reduced to players of bit-parts in another person's story.

Tribal stories

Stories are often told within groups of people who feel they relate closely to one another. The traditional image is of people gathered around a campfire telling each other stories, literally within the tribe. Views of the world in a tribe are maintained by storytelling, as they are within a family. The annual retelling of the Passover story in the Jewish tradition is one example of this. Views are formed within the tribe and the stories that are shared and retold express a particular view of the world which both makes the story comprehensible and is often reinforced by the story. People are more likely to develop views that are consistent with other members of the tribe than they are to develop contrasting views on the basis of information. The same is also true for any group of like-minded people within a church.

For this to work, there needs to be something about the story that is especially attractive to the members of the group. At the time of writing, in 2017, we have just seen two examples of stories that look very unconvincing to those outside of a tribe being accepted by those within the tribe. Just over half of those who voted in the UK referendum on whether to leave the EU voted to do so. And while the majority of voters in the US voted against Donald Trump, enough people voted for him to give him an unexpected win in the election for president. In both cases, people on the losing side are puzzled; how could it possibly be that so many people voted the other way? Supporters of one side in either of those elections, it turned out, barely knew anyone who voted the other way. They were ignorant of how those who were not members of their own tribe saw the world. In both cases, the winning side had a tribal slogan which gave a clearer story than the other side. Trump's 'Make America great again' appears meaningless to those who do not support him, but from the number of hats and T-shirts that bore that slogan, as well as from the result of the vote, it seems to have offered a story line with wide appeal. Similarly, the Brexit slogan of 'Take back control' seems to have been seen as a powerful, simple but convincing story by many voters, even if their opponents cannot see any sense in it, or what it might mean practically. If a story line appeals within the tribe, then that is enough. When one of the leaders of the Brexit campaign said that 'people have had enough of experts', this was heard as ridiculous and stupid by those who had voted the other way, and insightful by those who had voted with him! Stories can fall into more or less fertile ground depending on tribal divisions, and this is as true in churches as anywhere else. If your story is not going down well, or is failing to influence those whom you hoped to influence, have you paid attention to their tribal loyalties? This can lead to an echo effect, which we will discuss in the next section.

Stories and truth

Readers will have understood by now that, when we talk of stories, we are not talking about wild fantasies or about spin. Our argument is that the normal human condition is both to tell and to live stories. A story is subject to the same risks of falsehood as any other kind of communication. However, truth has become a very hot topic, with 'post-truth' having been voted word of the year in 2016. The possibility that people could be concealing falsehoods in their stories has always been with us, but the scale of the problem became apparent when the belief that Saddam Hussein, President of Iraq, had stockpiled 'weapons of mass destruction', which he intended to use against the West, was propagated by President George W. Bush of the United States, with the unlimited support of Prime Minister Tony Blair of the

United Kingdom. Both governments and their spokespeople declared their complete confidence in the story of weapons of mass destruction, but it gradually emerged that the intelligence reports had been much less definitive than originally claimed, and that parts of the supporting evidence had been plagiarized from elsewhere rather than being genuine reports from intelligence. As the story of weapons of mass destruction was undermined, as the war turned into a dirtier and more deadly affair, so public belief in the politicians who had led their countries into the war dwindled. Tony Blair went quite quickly from having been an unusually popular politician for a long time to being despised as the person who had taken reports that had been 'sexed up', made more clear and definitive than the evidence supported, and persuaded some citizens of his country to accept the story as the truth. Nyhan and Reiffler (2010) have shown that if you believe a story and you are presented with evidence in the opposite direction, it can actually lead you to believe even more strongly in the original story. We are prone to confirm and strengthen stories we believe in even if we are presented with opposing data. Research shows that brighter people, contrary to their own expectations, are even more prone to this bias!

The American satirist Stephen Colbert, pretending to be a right-wing commentator, coined the word 'truthiness' for when he was convinced of something 'in his guts', regardless of the evidence. Researchers in narratives have referred to 'narrative truths', which means something that comes across coherently within a story (Polkinghorne, 2007). If we see something working well in a story we take it as narrative truth. But some stories are not borne out by the facts. The debates around the election of Trump and the Brexit vote showed huge anger as people felt that other people, but not they themselves, had been misled into seeing unlikely opinions as 'facts'. They then became furious at the capacity of others to accept such lies. However, the evidence from recent cognitive studies suggests that the acceptance of something as 'the truth' is much more subjective than we have given it credit for (Fidgen, 2017). The political debates of the last few years mirror religious debates of previous centuries where people were prepared to kill each other over a disagreement as to what constituted truth.

There is even some evidence that people move to live in areas where more people think as they do, so that they can reinforce their views of the world in discussion with their neighbours. Given that, what are our chances of sorting out the truth of particular stories? The best evidence that we have not sealed ourselves into an echo chamber, where we only hear what we already believe and expect to hear, is that we change our minds. Changing our minds is another word for learning, even though it is sometimes mocked as 'doing a U turn'. Perhaps we should be more forgiving of ourselves and others when doing a U turn, and suspicious of anyone who lives in such a well-sealed echo chamber that they do not need to do them.

Stories and trust

We trust some people to tell us stories, and we are more wary of others. Working with the storying abilities of colleagues, allowing your organization to be filled with story, requires a considerable degree of trust on the part of those who are responsible for the organization. Storytelling can be a relatively tender plant, which will wither if it is not tended and nurtured. It is also very hard to control where stories take you. Sometimes a story can be carefully planned and directed, but very often this turns out to be unexciting and unconvincing. Donald Trump's capacity to tell stories that appeared to be straight from the heart (full of 'truthiness') with no sign of intervention from his brain was one of the factors that led to people trusting his stories and being influenced by them, even at the same time as they were appalled (and their attention was caught) by some aspects of both him and them.

Trust is not necessarily achieved by being trustworthy. We both worked at different times with an excellent, entertaining and witty storyteller, who was also brilliant intellectually. He would come into your office, take your elbow, and tell you a string of disgraceful stories about your colleagues, and you would both have a good laugh. You knew full well that, on leaving, he would be down the corridor telling equally disgraceful stories about you to another of those colleagues, possibly to the same one that you and he had just been laughing about. He was by any normal standards completely untrustworthy, and yet we all trusted him against our better judgement because we liked him. Part of this was because he was taking a risk by telling his stories. We could have done him damage by relaying his story back to the person he was talking about, so he had first trusted us with his scurrilous story. Trust is often returned with interest.

The clearest influence of trust on stories is whether you trust people to be able to tell their stories at all. Some clergy seem not to listen at all to the stories within their congregation, or if they do it is only to tell the storyteller that they have misunderstood things and got the story quite wrong. Fisk (2017) argued that Hillary Clinton could have won the 2016 US election if she had listened to Arab Americans, but, despite repeated attempts from within her campaign to get her to meet groups of them, she never prioritized this. Listening to people takes time, and one of the reasons we do not do it is that we wish to rush on to another activity. We show trust by giving people time to listen to them.

Mead (2014) argues that the changeability of stories is a crucial part of how they work. He quotes an anonymous source as saying, 'A story that can't change is as useful as a parachute that can't open.' Stories that are too fixed and permanent lose credibility. One of us once had to drive a futurologist from Bath to Heathrow for an evening session with some MBA students. On the journey, he told a number of stories, and told them well, with plenty of life and action. On the return journey he retold the same stories, including the same apparently improvised incidentals. Stories that had been credible to start with lost credibility when it became obvious how well rehearsed and unchanging they were. Mead (2014) also quotes Salman Rushdie as saying:

> Those who do not have power over the story that dominates their lives, the power to retell it, rethink it, deconstruct it, joke about it, and change it as times change, truly are powerless because they cannot think new thoughts. (p. 113)

Mead says that the core of his argument is that, 'whereas information and argument both ask us to agree with them, stories make no such demand. Instead, they offer us vicarious experiences that invite our sympathy and understanding' (2014, p. 87). We trust stories by getting involved in them, not by giving intellectual assent to them. However, as Parry and Hansen (2007) say, 'A story cannot champion itself . . . Stories cannot defend themselves against restorying' (p. 292). Stories cannot survive without tellers. Once the story is in circulation, retelling can be done by others as the story gets told and retold through the organization. A challenge for people who are new to senior roles is to understand the extent to which stories will be told about them. They may need to think not only about what they did and what they intended in the way of consequences, but also about the way others will tell their own stories about these events. Parry and Hansen (2007) also point out that stories are often challenged by other stories. Two people come out of a meeting with different stories about what happened in it. These two stories are retold in the organization and compete with each other, until one of them becomes the predominant story.

Golemon (2010a) emphasizes the need for leaders to trust the stories of others:

> Learning to trust that the religious tradition or congregational history will hold if reworked by the community at large, including newcomers, is one of the goals that performative practices can engender. The more that pastors, priests, and rabbis are coached in taking on the story of Scripture or tradition as their own story, the more they will begin to trust others around them to do the same. (p. 23)

Anyone who seeks a monopoly of storytelling in their church is dangerous. In a healthy church, in our view, one person tells some stories and then steps back to listen to others' stories, without any presumption that their own stories were the most important ones. Conversation works by people trading stories. If you tell stories, you expect others to reciprocate with theirs. If you don't listen to them, or if you tell them that they have got it all wrong, that they misunderstand their own stories, those stories are likely to dry up. If you listen to them they may well listen to themselves with more care and improve their skills of telling stories in the church, and thus they are developed as narrative leaders. So the question for leaders in churches, and particularly for religious professionals, is, do you want others in the church to develop as narrative leaders? You will not get your own way so easily in future if they do, but you will be living in a more vibrant and vital community.

The ecology of stories

For our final take on multiple stories we use ideas and phrases from the work of Gabriel (2016). Gabriel shows that master narratives in organizations, the stories told by the most powerful, do not come to life as narratives until there are counter-narratives, the different stories that come from less powerful people, for them to contest with. They also travel – stories are no respecters of organizational boundaries. But, rather akin to the point above about stories that do not change not really being stories, if there is no counter-story and thus no invitation for people to make yet more interesting stories out of the master story, the master story dies. Interest can only be retained by stories that are part of some contest. Gabriel goes on from this to a system of narrative ecologies, describing different ways that groups of stories can live with each other.

Gabriel identifies *narrative temperate regions*, where lots of things can grow, where stories are profuse and varied, and where storytellers are fairly tolerant of one another. This would be the case in socially complex and diverse places, and where people felt reasonably free to tell their own stories. Many stories can flourish in the temperate region, because these are very healthy regions in terms of their nourishing of diverse stories, but they are not easy places to control or to plan. The 'planned' church, with its mission statements, strategies and so on, may not want to be a narrative temperate region, because that sounds too chaotic for the taste of the senior management.

Then there are *narrative deserts*, where only a few narratives can grow, and they are relatively scratty, struggling affairs. In the narrative desert the struggle for stories to survive is not because of the competition from other stories, but instead is because of a harsh environment which is not conducive to the survival of any story. There may be a taboo against stories, or it may be that the connections between people are not strong and trusting enough to promote the telling and hearing of stories.

Then there are *narrative monocultures*, places where there are some stories around, but they are all very similar. These places lack counter-narratives, and fit in well with a totalitarian organization. There are certainly churches like this, where everyone tells very much the same story and where any other story struggles to survive. Think of a field of wheat, a monoculture, where any weeds (counter-narratives) are very obvious, and will be torn out quickly. Then imagine an insecure, anxious church where house-group leaders are reporting back on any inappropriate stories from their members, who will then be told why they are wrong. At the extreme, this becomes a cult.

Narrative mountains can grow only a few feeble stories which cling on but show no vigour. Gabriel applies the term particularly to loosely structured places that meet only occasionally to do a particular task, but do not have enough life of their own for strong narratives to take root. No one cares enough about these environments to lavish their narrative energy on them. Think the local branch of 'Churches Together', or the Diocesan Synod.

Narrative marshlands are also often networks rather than structured organizations. In the marshland many stories can grow and develop, but they risk sinking into the mud. The culture of stories is rich, but they do not necessarily survive all that long. This could be the realm of the task group or ad hoc committee, which meets, tells plenty of stories, and reaches a conclusion at which point the group has done its job, so the stories are not preserved. Sadly, those setting up such groups are not usually interested in collecting and preserving those stories, so the narrative richness is quickly lost and absorbed into the peat bog.

Narrative jungles are a little like temperate regions, but hotter, with everything growing faster and competing more openly for light and space. They are dangerous places, with strange animals lurking in the undergrowth, and all sorts of wild stories being told – conspiracy theories, gossip about other people, alongside benevolent stories which could bear good fruit. They are hard to control, although, because of the sheer profusion of stories and the potential threat, it may be that much easier for an authoritarian to take charge of them, as people begin to look for clarity amid the chaos.

Narrative allotments or gardens are where people grow their own private collection of narratives, carefully protecting them from counter-narratives. People's stories are treated with great interest and concern, and listened to carefully. The atmosphere on the allotment is warm and loving, and conflict is rare. At this point we might conclude that Gabriel has never owned an allotment, but never mind, we can see what he means by the metaphor. Narrative allotments work well if the objective is comfort, not so well if the development of better stories and an organization that learns are the objective. Narrative allotments can be planned and controlled, and the owner can keep up with the weeding.

Stories are generally more like gardening than like sculpture. Many of the popular management techniques of 20 years ago, which are still being brought into the church, are like subtractive sculpture. You chip things off a block of stone or wood until you think it is the right shape. This does not fit with many people's experiences of organizations, where you plant, water, weed, prune and so on, but you are never fully in control. The gardener cannot cause the growth. The best thing they can do is to try to give the plant as good a chance as they can to find its own pattern of growth.

Questions

1 Where do the stories that people tell most readily tend to be located in a church that you know: the gospel, the building, the congregation or the denomination? Why?
2 Are there different storytelling tribes in your church? Do they ever get to hear one another's stories?
3 Which of the storytelling ecologies characterizes a church that you know? Is anyone trying to influence or change those ecologies, and if so, how are they getting on?

5

Who Owns the Story?

The ownership of stories is contested and difficult. Stories do not behave as you might hope that private property would. You tell stories and, at the same time, your stories tell you. They are not always the kind of thing you can shape and control. They take on a life of their own. As many novelists have commented, they take twists that you had not intended when you started to tell them. In the act of telling, your understanding of your story and its meaning changes. The point you had meant to illustrate, and for which you chose the story, suddenly becomes open to question.

At other times they behave much more placidly and predictably. But we suggest that, if you consider your own experience of storytelling, the times when stories are out of control, when they refuse to be disciplined, are also the times when they are most exciting and of most interest to you and to others. We almost need another word – ditties, perhaps? – for those little stories that lack a life of their own. Meanwhile, for most of this book, when we refer to 'leading by story' we are talking of the kind of active, vigorous story that tells you as much as you are telling it. In this chapter we will talk about some of the suggestions that have been made about how we can improve our ability to lead with story. We then go back a stage to ask whether there is any other realistic way of leading in any case. Perhaps there is no option other than to lead with stories, and if we fail to do so the only result will be that someone else supplies stories and leads with them instead.

We often work with an individualistic model of action as well as of storytelling, but there are some interesting ways in which thinking more carefully about how stories work in churches takes us into the nature of collective processes that go beyond the individual.

We shall look at the idea that hearing stories requires a degree of humility and hospitality. As Denning (2011a) puts it, 'the hard part of communication is often figuring out what story the audience is currently living' (p. 89). If you think you know what someone is going to say, you may well not be listening enough to hear their story. Finally, we shall consider the idea that leading is about curating stories, selecting the ones that are displayed and the story that is told in how they are displayed.

How to lead with stories

Parry (2008) has a number of suggestions about how people best lead with stories. He deliberately works with the idea of 'story-making' rather than 'story-writing' because he thinks the latter sounds too instrumental. So he does not mean this as a checklist of things you can do to make sure that your story prevails, so much as a set of characteristics of a story that best reflect leadership.

First, he says, make it a plausible story. Does this story come across to the hearers as one that could actually happen? Importantly, this plausibility is in the world of the hearer, not that of the teller. That someone else finds it plausible, or even that you know it actually took place, is not the point. The other side of plausibility is that it needs some novelty, something surprising or interesting enough about it for the hearer to notice the story; total plausibility could shade into boring invisibility.

Second, give all people a part in the story. Does the overall story being told offer something that excites the interest of lots of people, and offer them a meaningful way of feeling part of it? Does it suggest that this is something worth caring about, something worth dropping other activities for? If a story is too prescriptive and detailed it may be hard for people to see their place in it, or why they are needed. A great story will be one where others hear it and immediately see a place in it that they could occupy, a character that they could be. The injunction we have referred to more than once before to 'see what God is doing, and join in' is a good example of a way of telling a story that invites others to find their own end of a story and be led by it. This has implications for the sort of story that will work well. For example, stories that require the efforts of one heroic person may offer only one role. Stories that require the involvement of the whole people of God, and recognize that there will be a diversity of the gifts that those people can bring, can offer as many roles as there are people, or more. However, it is interesting how reluctant many of us are to tell stories that show us to be dependent or needy. We want to tell stories that show that we are doing fine and are in control of the situation. If we do that, we will tell stories in which we do not need anyone else to take a part.

Third, give them power. Having a part in the story is important, but people are more likely to join in fully if they can also see a way in which they can be influential within the story in their own right. If you can tell a story in such a way that the members of the church can be powerful actors within the story, even if only in a minor way, they will not need to find other stories to join in with to exercise power. If there are too many people hanging around with no story to join in with, the scene is set for other stories to arise and for people to find themselves roles in those stories. Some of those alternative stories could end up being productive – for example, they could lead to the birthing of a new house group; but they could equally be destructive – they could be the group that decides to threaten a church with a schism. You will not necessarily want to encourage all stories, but a vacuum of roles in stories will probably not last long – someone will fill it with a new story and new opportunities. You cannot control stories but you can decide whether you want to leave a vacuum that invites someone else to offer opportunities for the congregation's unmet ambitions. As we said in Chapter 2, Parry also suggests that the reason Martin Luther King's story line was in the end more attractive to black Americans than Malcolm X's was that Martin Luther King offered black people an equal role in his dominant story; Malcolm X said they were disempowered and had to seize power. That is a much less attractive narrative, so it lost out.

Fourth, have a 'moral' to the story. Parry picks up the ideas of Boje (2001) on 'antenarrative' – the list of events which has not yet been turned into a story. An antenarrative could be seen as a kit from which a story can be made, but one of the things it crucially lacks is a moral, a point. Why does anyone want to be a part of this story? So what difference would it make if this story never happened? Participants are always looking to make sense of the way they spend their limited lifetimes and their bounded energy. They want to be able to find a meaning that they can be happy with. Of course the moral of the story does not necessarily have to be a good one; the moral could be 'this will make lots of money' or 'this will really hurt some people'. We are not making judgements here about what constitutes a good moral, but rather saying that there has to be some point to the activity in the story. However, Parry believes that the leader has to take responsibility for the moral in the story, and not leave everyone to find their own moral in it: 'If one leaves it to the audience to work out the moral of the story, the risk is that a dysfunctional meaning might be concluded' (p. 142). As Mead (2017) argues, leading is a way of making meaning with, and sometimes for, people.

Fifth, the story should have a happy ending. Not necessarily an 'and they all lived happily ever after' type ending. The happy ending may be one in which tensions are unresolved and there is plenty more story still to live, but the overall outcome needs to be optimistic. Otherwise it does not give the sense of having arrived at its destination; if the outcome is not positive, we think we are at a staging post of the story rather than at the end. We are not fully clear in our own minds as to whether we agree with Parry on this last point, and we are still playing with examples and counter-examples, but we offer this to our readers as an example of a story that you will need to complete for yourselves!

Stories are inevitable

Never mind whose story it is, why do you refer to what we are talking about as a 'story' anyhow? When I go into schools with 'Open the Book' the kids tell me that Christianity is all just stories, whereas the Muslim religion is all about facts.

This view came, with some anger, from a lay church leader when she heard from one of us that we were working on a book on leading by story in churches. Of course we hope that we have explained ourselves better by this stage of the book, but it is worth revisiting the relationship between stories and events. When we tell someone about something that happened, we tell a story about it. Stories are neither more nor less true than any other form of communication. A story about an event is always incomplete, just as a scientific account of an experiment is always incomplete. It is not possible to include everything that happened in your account of the event. There are too many possible perspectives, too many other concomitant events which are probably nothing to do with it – but that is a judgement call. A story is always going to be a selective account, selected to convey the meaning that the story-teller sees in the event being described, and selected to help the hearers make a particular kind of sense out of the event. To go back to our description of Boje (2001) above, events form the antenarrative, the raw material from which stories are constructed. These events are then infused with meaning and made memorable by being related as a story.

You might like to take the biblical story of Ruth and strip it back to its antenarrative, the list of events that takes place. Not difficult to do, although it is difficult to persuade oneself to put the time and energy into doing it, because we are used to the story and the way it makes sense of the events in the antenarrative. But it will illustrate the point, because it shows that other stories could have been told from that antenarrative, and that the story we know is thoroughly bound up with how we now make sense of it. Other stories could have been told, but this does not mean that the story we all know is not the truth, or that it would be somehow more objective to list the events without the story.

Stories will always get told about events. The choice that church members have is not whether stories will or will not be told about what is going on in their churches, but only whether they wish to be involved in the telling, or whether they would rather leave this to others. Stories are what gives meaning to events, so it seems clear that those who wish to be involved in leadership in churches will be the ones who tell the stories and thus offer meaning to others around them. How could someone who wishes to be involved in leadership not wish to be the storyteller?

Czarniawska (1997) takes this idea further: 'Organizational stories capture organizational life in a way that no compilation of facts ever can; this is because they are carriers of life itself, not just "reports" on it' (p. 21). The life of the organization is in the meaning given to events by stories. Thus the stories go beyond being reports of events and how events can be understood, and become the essence of life.

Fentress-Williams (2010) points out very engagingly that one can often have an official story (for example what is in your c.v.) and an unofficial story (for example the stories that your siblings tell about you if asked). She also gives the example of the 'self-made man' whose spouse has worked long and hard in obscurity to enable his success, and she contrasts this with the scriptural practice of often giving us both the official and the unofficial versions of the story alongside each other (for example, the story of David and Bathsheba). Just as this section has argued that the telling of stories is inevitable, it is also true that the telling of several, to some extent conflicting, stories is inevitable except in totalitarian regimes. Different stories, unofficial stories and counter-stories are the normal currency of organizational life. At times this may irritate the person who sees themselves as the leader whose influence should be accepted, the person to whom authority has been given by God or the church, but they should get over it. The counter-stories, the funny stories that reveal the feet of clay of the charismatic leader, are also part of the God-given narrative mix, and people flourish much more in a mixed economy of stories than they do in a regimented, unitary story.

Stories go beyond the individual

The benefits of polyvocal organizations have been emphasized in recent work (Boje, 2008; Steyaert and van Looy, 2010). There has been a recognition that not enough different voices have been influencing the direction of organizations, and that the effectiveness of organizations is the loser when there is too little variety in the voices that are heard. Stories are beneficial in this because they seem to lend themselves naturally to polyvocality. Stories generate counter-stories, they get passed round and passed on, they give a lot of people a way of saying things. Stories can also be multi-authored in the sense that one person will start to tell them and then another person will pick up the story part way through, take it further, and then hand it on to someone else. Within families or workgroups who know each other well this can be a common procedure, and another way of enabling polyvocality (Boje, 1991). There can often be a role for someone to help a congregation shape a story, and Peers (2010) suggests that this can be the moment to choose not to support a problem-oriented story (the problem we have got here is that there are just no young people living in this area, or whatever), and instead to help co-author a new story; 'our role shifts to being a midwife to a new vision' (p. 45).

Stories do not just reflect togetherness; they also produce it. Listening to stories together is an ancient human form of fellowship, symbolized by the well-loved myth of our ancestors sitting by the campfire at night listening to the tribal stories that we were discussing in Chapter 4. In order for this to work, there has to be a degree of putting others' stories before your own, of depriving the world, briefly, of your own wisdom. While we are listening to others' stories we will miss out on the opportunity to tell stories that put us in a good light. Standish (2007) says that you can never be the hero of the story. This needs some thinking about. Some of the most popular books about church leadership are written by people who are not arrogant, who are seeking to be the best they can as leaders in churches, but who are certainly portrayed as heroes in their own stories (Warren, 1995; Hybels, 2002). The whole tradition of testimony in some churches is about telling stories of which you are the hero, even if that tradition demands that you present more as the villain. And surely we need to develop our capacity to hear our own stories as well as those of others? We will come back to these questions.

Moschella (2010) goes so far as to say that teaching students on ministry courses to be ethnographers can be a really important part of their formation. The act of respectful listening and honest engagement in what others in the church are saying is not something that comes naturally to many ministers (or others). Experts want to exercise the skills in which they have gained expertise. If you have a skill you probably feel called to make the most of it, to display it often for the good of all, and not to hide it away while you are listening to others. Moschella argues that, for just these reasons, listening for the stories of others is a valuable part of pastoral development; getting to hear the stories is a bonus that comes along with the better listening.

Bakan (1966) was responsible for bringing the notions of agency and communion into psychological discourse. People in organizations do things. They show agency. Other people interact with them and value them because they do things. Organizations are active places, and the doing is important. Some of those things are well worth doing! However, it is equally true that people are 'being' in organizations, which is what Bakan means by communion. We are concerned not only with each other's actions, but also with who the other person is, what their being is, what is going on for them. The view of people as either do-ers or be-ers has often been seen as quite a fundamental difference in approach between the activist, instrumental view of the person and the contemplative approach that emphasizes their personal value. But Bakan argues that story-telling brings these two views together. In stories, people do things, and that action is part of the topic of the storytelling. Stories, however, are equally interested in the being and the internal world of the character who is acting, and stories can be an excellent way of hearing about this.

The humility of hearing stories

Throughout this book, there is a theme about stories and humility which we have brought to the surface only occasionally. Others' stories are very easy to come by. People are willing and sometimes all too willing to tell you their stories. Stories are not generally difficult to understand. So why would not everybody who wants to contribute to the leadership of their churches listen to the stories of their fellow members, and understand where they are coming from? What could be easier?

It is true that most people have the skills to be able to do this, but it is demanding for the listener. Much of the time in conversation our attention is so taken up with planning what we are going to say next that we are scarcely listening to what the other person is saying. Listening to the stories of others requires a level of humility that does not just happen. As Mead (2017) points out, listening can be painful. If you really listen to what someone is saying, you risk being changed by what you hear. Johnston (2010) associates story sharing with hospitality, and both of them with leadership. She talks about being welcomed into a community very different from most of her experience, and about how they told her the stories they thought she needed to know in order to understand their lives. The association between sharing stories and hospitality is a good one. Stories are often best shared over food and drink, and creating a congenial venue for this is what hospitality is all about. For Christians, the Eucharist is a concentrated example.

Hearing stories can not only be painful and require us to be open to change, but is also quite simply very hard work. Hours of careful listening do not come without great effort on the part of the listener. Part of this is the effort to keep ourselves from bad habits of half listening while planning our own next sentence – and thus not really listening at all. More interestingly, there is the knock-on effect of hearing others' stories. Sally Fox, in her interview with Geoff Mead (Mead, 2017), comments that, by hearing others' stories, we can see what needs to emerge in our own. This is one of the ways in which active story listening changes us. When we hear stories, we make our own connections with what we are being told. When two individuals tell each other stories with real listening, the process is no longer really individual. It is a process of mutual influence and mutual change. Ramsey (2010) suggests that part of the difference is that people who are telling each other stories are forced really to look at each other. If you have struggled to tell a story to someone whose attention was difficult to hold, you will know what this feels like. Telling a story to an attentive listener, a listener who you can see being affected and influenced by the story as you tell it, is a remarkable experience. Both teller and hearer are very susceptible to the influence of the other under conditions of close listening.

It is worth thinking about why storytelling sometimes does not feel like this. Storytelling is sometimes done as a performance which does not expect, or even really allow, this kind of active response from the listener. Sometimes it is done as a performance rather than an invitation. The hearers are supposed to be impressed, to applaud, to admire, but not to participate and certainly not to change the storyteller. The teller believes they have the right to control the story, to take it where they wish. The autonomy either of the listener or of the story itself does not seem to concern them. Our suggestion is that we can all sense when we think this is the case, when storytelling is being done in a way which we are supposed to acquiesce in passively, and that this form of storytelling, while it can be entertaining, is not as likely to influence us as the more participatory forms.

As we mentioned in Chapter 2, this is taken a stage further by Parry and Hansen (2007):

> We transcend the notion that leaders tell stories, to the proposition that stories themselves operate like leaders. We suggest that people follow the story as much as they follow the storyteller or author, hence the story becomes the leader. In discussing the characteristics that stories share with leadership, we generate two propositions. First, within the context of organizational development, leadership development can move from 'people' development to the development of the narratives that resonate within organizations. Second, we decouple leader as person or position, from leadership as process in order to illustrate stories as leaders. (p. 281)

In other words, the story works best when it has a measure of independence from the person who is telling it. It becomes more powerful as it is associated more with the interaction between teller and hearer, as the story itself, rather than as a carrier of a power relationship. It becomes more powerful when, in the phrase from Barthes (1974) that we referred to in Chapter 2, it is more 'writerly' than 'readerly', that is, when it invites the hearer into a more active role as a co-writer of the story, rather than expecting them to sit back as a passive reader.

Curating the stories

We influence the stories that people can tell by the way we listen to them and respond. Some people and situations make it really easy for you to get into telling your story, others make it feel really difficult for you to tell your story. One of us was once telling a story at an academic conference about a piece of data in our research. It was a very entertaining story that we had been told by one of our research subjects about the early days of research on Viagra, and how interest in the drug had risen rapidly when one of the first researchers had demonstrated live at a conference how effective the drug was. The story was well tested, and has been confirmed to us by several of those who were at the original presentation. It was one we had told several times, and had always worked well in conveying something about how ideas get on to the agenda of communities (which was the topic of our research). On this occasion, however, the audience listened in stony silence. For some reason we had not managed to take them with us, and the lack of response from some people seemed to be infectious and very deflating to us.

This experience is fortunately rare but we expect most readers will recognize it. There are places where it becomes really difficult to tell a particular type of story. Similarly, there are times when stories of a particular type are welcomed and encouraged. It is quite possible for people to make it easier or harder for others to tell a story. A smile and a nod will encourage, while a sigh and losing eye contact will discourage. We encourage a climate that nurtures some stories rather than others. Those with influence and respect in their communities act as curators for stories, encouraging some to be displayed rather than others, and arranging the context of the display so as to give extra meaning to the stories, in the same way as the curator of an exhibition both selects the objects to display and then arranges the display to make it more meaningful than the objects would be separately.

Parry and Hansen (2007) suggest five practical messages that could help those who are leading narratively in their organizations. First, they should be aware of the stories that are circulating, and they should notice which of these stories are supportive to individuals or the organization, and which of them are undermining. Above all, they should be conscious of these stories, and take their effects seriously, never dismissing them as 'just stories'.

Second, with the negative and damaging stories that are circulating, they should be ready to take those stories and turn them into positive stories. For an individual-level example of this, Cynthia Bourgeault (2004) tells the story of Thomas Keating leading a session for a group of nuns on centring prayer. One of the nuns tells him after the session that she will never be able to do what he is recommending, because in a 20-minute session she had 10,000 thoughts. 'How lovely!' responded Thomas Keating without missing a beat. 'Ten thousand opportunities to return to God!' (p. 24). The negative story has been quickly and effectively put into a context that turns it into a positive story.

Third, those who in any way move or shake in organizations need to be aware that everything they do can become a story, which will be told and retold by others. If this is not happening, if no stories are being told about them, it is most unlikely that they are exercising any leadership. Some people feel that such awareness of the stories you generate is over self-conscious, even a little narcissistic. We would argue that it is no more manipulative than the way in which we take care of how we express ourselves to people who we think might be hurt by careless words on our part. Jesus was prepared to eat and drink with the disreputable, but then he was also prepared to deal with the narrative consequences of this when people suggested that he was eating and drinking with sinners because he did not realize that they were sinners. We should not be surprised to find that our actions have become others' stories.

Fourth, and in a way that we find reminiscent of modern curating practices for hands-on exhibitions, Parry and Hansen (2007) say:

> [T]he better stories for leadership are those that represent the collective organization, where everyone gets to participate in the discourse that creates stories. Rather than building prescriptive stories into one's discourse, individuals could allow followers to be empowered when determining how to write or enact the story. (p. 296)

This is reminiscent of our point earlier in the chapter about 'writerly' stories, the ones where the listeners are invited to join in the crafting and writing of the story, thus sharing in the leading, while also diminishing the degree of control exercised by the formal leader.

Fifth, we can let go of the expectation that leaders will always want to advertise their own importance and effectiveness to others. This has become something of a leadership cliché, with the expectation that pomposity and self-aggrandisement will impress others, and that continual talk about one's own effectiveness is an important part of showing confidence as a leader. While this may be a belief that is held by some appointing committees and some candidates, French and Simpson (2011) note that several of the leaders of large organizations who they talk to in their research do not talk like this at all. Instead, they downplay the importance of leadership, questioning how useful a concept it is, and whether it justifies the rarefied status it is often given. This fits with our own observations too, where sometimes the most effective leaders have told us that they think that the very idea that they are specially gifted, and that they know what they are doing as leaders, even that they are somehow in control, is a comforting illusion for their followers. We attribute great skill and strategic wisdom to people whom we describe as leaders in order to feel less insecure about our future and the future of our churches. This may make us feel comfortable, but does it reflect anything more than our desire to hand over responsibility to someone else? Is it both unhealthy and unfair to cast our leaders as heroes when they know that they are limited, human, and not able to deliver all the outcomes they would like?

Standish (2010) emphasizes the crafting of the story rather than the curating of it:

> [G]reat leaders seem to craft a story, a story that inspires others in the organization, team or congregation so that they willingly become a part of and live out this story in their work and lives (p. 70) . . . One of the talents of great narrative leaders is that they see plotlines and possibilities that others do not. (p. 74)

This links up the storytelling activity of leadership with the concept of curating stories. When someone curates an exhibition, they are placing the objects in the exhibition into a story. The objects take up the role of Boje's antenarrative. They are like events that have not yet been turned into a story. The art of curating is not only the selection of objects, but the creation of a story that puts those objects together, that turns them into a narrative. So curating is itself a way of crafting the story, both by the selection and encouragement of some elements of the story, and in giving a plot line to the way that the elements of the stories are seen together.

Questions

1 Which of Parry's four points (plausibility, giving everyone a part, empowerment and a moral) about how to lead with stories do you think is the most crucial?

2 How can we balance ideas about the humility of hearing stories with the need to be open about what we think, and with our need to hear our own stories too?

3 Think of an example that you have seen of someone acting as a curator of stories. What made them good or bad at the role?

6

Church Narratives: Interpretive Stories

Introduction

So far we have explored the nature of leadership and how that relates to the place of stories and storytelling in organizations. We have discussed the role of narrative in churches and in the next three chapters we shall examine that in detail. Given the role of story and parable within Scripture, there is surprisingly little work on their place within contemporary churches. Probably the best-known analysis is James F. Hopewell's *Congregation: Stories and structures* (1987) which remains a seminal text.

John Pritchard has been influenced by Hopewell's work and by story generally (Pritchard, 2001). There is some helpful discussion on the importance of story in the final chapter of *Managing God's Business* (2005) by Malcolm Torry; and Larry A. Golemon has edited a series of three short books on narrative leadership and congregational change with the overall title of the *Narrative Leadership Collection* (2010), which we have referred to extensively in Chapters 3, 4 and 5. In addition, one of us has written a brief introduction to the role of narrative in church ministry (Roberts, 2017), but the present book is the first full-scale study since Hopewell's and the first to bring together the latest ideas from the world of narrative leadership and apply them to churches.

From a personal and professional perspective, we have been observing the role that stories play in churches for many years both jointly and independently. We have worked together in one church (Christ Church, Bath) in the roles of priest and director of music, but also have wide experience of how churches function in different contexts. In these three chapters we shall be considering stories in churches under three headings, (1) Interpretive stories, (2) Identity stories, and (3) Improvised stories, each of which has a number of sub-genres. The interpretive stories are the 'big picture' narratives that frame the work and mission of the church. In particular we identify three areas of storytelling that are vital in this process: (1) Theological narratives, (2) Ecclesial narratives, and (3) Liturgical narratives. In Chapter 7 we will examine the various identity stories in more detail, while Chapter 8 will address the numerous improvised stories in churches. Following that we offer a case study of how a traditional consultancy intervention in a church interacts with a narrative framework. Then in our conclusion we will draw together some recommendations for the practice of storytelling and church leadership.

We shall outline briefly the three sub-genres of interpretive story before turning to examine each in detail, building on our discussion of the locus of stories in Chapter 4.

1 Theological narratives

These are the communal stories which encompass the wide range of Christian 'Godtalk' being told and rehearsed within churches, which shape how the outside world is perceived as well as framing many of the internal conflicts. For instance, the theological stories told by Anglicans and Catholics about the nature of authority in those two churches have similarities but also some significant differences (for example, the way in which they tell the story of the Reformation or their narratives about atonement). An important element in any discussion regarding authority will be the Bible and what weight is given to the different ways of interpreting the texts in Scripture.

2 Ecclesial narratives

These are the narratives told by different churches about their own organizational autobiographies. So, although Methodism and the

Church of England are close siblings, the stories they tell about themselves and each other unavoidably shape their interactions (or lack of them). Of course this narrative strand goes back much further – not only through the whole history of the Church, back to the New Testament, but beyond that. In the introduction to his account of Christianity, Diarmaid MacCulloch writes of having 'two thousand years' worth of *Christian* stories to tell' (MacCulloch, 2009, p. 1). Yet even that feat of storytelling has an earlier genesis: 'The story must therefore begin more than a millennium *before* Jesus, among the ancient Greeks and the Jews, two races which alike thought that they had a uniquely privileged place in the world's history' (MacCulloch, 2009, p. 2). The story of the people of God and the organization of the Church is a long and complex one.

3 Liturgical narratives

Churches and congregations rehearse their theological, ecclesial and other stories through their liturgy. Those churches that have a weekly Eucharist focused on an altar and those that have a weekly Service of the Word or Praise Worship focused on a projector screen are saying something very different about their understanding of the Church and its mission. One philosopher and theologian who has written extensively about the storied nature of liturgy in the Church and in non-ecclesial culture is James K. A. Smith (Smith, 2009, 2013). He observes:

> Liturgies are compressed, repeated, performed narratives that, over time, conscript us into the story they 'tell' by showing, by performing. Such orientating narratives are not explicitly 'told' in a 'once-upon-a-time' discursive mode . . . these stories are more like dramas that are enacted and performed. (Smith, 2013, p. 109)

What Is the Church?

It will be helpful at this stage to consider the question: What do we mean by Church/church? In essence, we shall be using 'church' to

denote local congregations that are self-consciously part of a denomination (for example Church of England, Methodist, Catholic);
gatherings of Christians that are equally self-consciously independent of established ecclesial identities (for example Hillsong, New
Wine, Mars Hill); or those that fall somewhere in between (for
example a 'fresh expression' or a franchise of another church such
as Holy Trinity, Brompton).

By contrast, we use 'Church' for the theological construct of the
Body of Christ, the worldwide Christian community and Church
in its largest sense. Theological notions of the Church are also
many and varied. Some writers use paradox to describe it, such
as Farley's 'The peculiarity of ecclesia is that it is a *determinate*
religious community *without boundaries*' (Farley, 1975, p. 171 –
our italics). Others use communal language, for example viewing the Church as a 'community of practice', as do Marsh, 2006,
and Fitzmaurice, 2016, both drawing upon the work of Etienne
Wenger. Others again use a typology, such as Coakley (2013) who
uses Max Weber's and Ernest Troeltsch's ideas about Christianity
in church, sect and mystical forms.[1]

We take theological and sociological descriptions of the Church
and churches seriously and have found them crucial in our analyses
of their life and work. However, in this book we are approaching them from a different angle, one that we think has enormous
potential but has been under-utilized by the Church and churches
themselves. Seeing the Body of Christ and its individual parts as
storytelling communities or story-sharing organizations opens up a
way of understanding that has been surprisingly under-appreciated,
especially given the importance of story and parable in Jesus' own
ministry and teaching.

In his analysis of the processes of organizational sensemaking
Karl Weick argues:

> [A] good story, like a workable cause map, shows patterns that
> may already exist in puzzles an actor now faces, or patterns that
> could be created anew in the interest of more order and sense in
> the future. The stories are templates. They are products of pre-
> vious efforts at sensemaking. They explain. And they energize.
> (Weick, 1995, p. 61)

Figure 1 places the Church/church at the heart of a number of 'good stories' which explain, create order and energize. In this chapter we look at three key interpretive stories that frame the Church's self-understanding and its perceptions of the wider world – theology, liturgy and ecclesiology – before exploring the different genres of identity stories (Chapter 7) and improvised stories (Chapter 8).

While we explore this narrative ecology and how the various storied 'flora' interact, as well as describing their relationships we will map them out using the diagram in Figure 1, which develops over the next two chapters. Although the theological, liturgical and ecclesial stories are depicted here as discrete, as in any ecology there is interaction and cross-pollination. The arrows in our

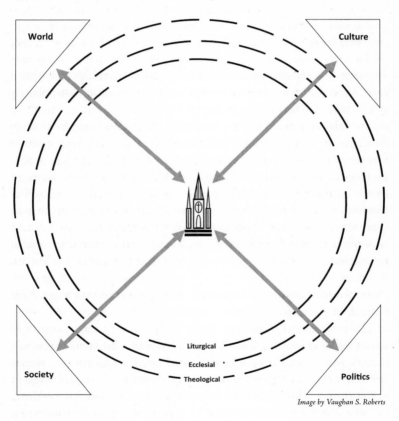

Image by Vaughan S. Roberts

Figure 1: Interpretive Stories.

diagram indicate this dynamic relationship, and that will increase when we add in the subsequent identity and improvised narratives. In Chapter 4 we set out Gabriel's narrative ecology and noted that gardeners cannot cause the growth. The best thing they can do is to try to give the plant as good a chance as they can to find its own pattern of growth. These three chapters aim to identify some of the plants that are growing in many church gardens so that those who lead and enable the stories can better understand the varieties of narrative that they will encounter.

We turn to the three forms of story under discussion in this chapter to ask: What are theological, ecclesial and liturgical narratives?

What are theological narratives?

At the start of an episode of the BBC TV programme *The Big Questions* aired to mark the four hundredth anniversary of Shakespeare's death, the TV producer Richard Denton was asked: 'Is there more truth and understanding of the human condition for you in Shakespeare or the Bible?' And he replied: 'The Bible tends to have lots of prescriptions and commandments but it doesn't say things that are recognizable to us now . . . The Bible tells you what to think and Shakespeare tells you, "Think".'[2] And this common perception of Scripture as merely a series of rules and requirements was repeated a number of times by other speakers. Something similar is popularly believed about the notion of theology and doctrine. In his introduction to the place of silence within the Church Diarmaid MacCulloch observes how human beings are pattern-making creatures and adds: 'Inflexible pattern-makers get very angry when their patterns are under threat' (MacCulloch, 2013, p. 4).

More often than not, it is those who resist change within the Church that colour the perceptions of those outside. Thus, theology can also be perceived as inflexible and rigid. Story and non-story form a crucial thread in MacCulloch's retelling of how Christian theology has been formed and challenged, and how this sometimes led to change within the Church or silencing of the protagonists. He traces patterns of silence through the Psalms and the Prophets, through Jesus and Paul, exploring how it is presented in those narratives. We can do something similar with many other biblical themes and ideas, because they are much more than 'prescriptions and commandments'. They are living stories which are reworked and retold over a long period of time.

For instance, in his book on church leadership Jackson W. Carroll draws attention to the importance of metaphor in Scripture and how images such as salt, light, household, clay jars, people of God, and royal priesthood have shaped Christian self-understanding. He particularly focuses on the how the 'Body of Christ' functions as a crucial organizational metaphor. This is achieved through its narrative potency, so the character and calling as Christ's body 'are defined by the story of Jesus: his life, ministry, death, and resurrection'.

> His story is central to all else that can be said about the church. When the church is faithful to its calling, it finds its life and direction in this narrative. The narrative shapes the church's identity, what it believes and what it practices; likewise, it shapes the exercise of authority and leadership in the church. (Carroll, 2011, p. 72)

Interestingly, Stephen Denning in his book on storytelling and leadership, intended for a secular readership, includes an analysis of Jesus' parables as an example of how stories have the power to ask sharp questions and convey complex values (Denning, 2011b, pp. 143–4).

At one level this clear connection between the story of Jesus' life and contemporary stories seems very straightforward. However, this form of interpretive story points to a distinctive feature of organizational narrative within the Church – its long and complex history. This was reflected in a conversation that one of us had with Jeffrey John, Dean of St Albans, about the story of his cathedral. He immediately referred back to the death of the first Christian martyr in Britain, St Alban, at the end of the third century. Ann Morisy tells a tale of meeting some Russian visitors to Britain and explaining how she was employed by the Diocese of London, which was founded in AD 604. Her listeners were amazed and that led her to reflect: 'They were right to look askance. It is rare to come across an organization that can trace its roots back 300 years and to find one that goes back well over 1,000 years is quite extraordinary' (Morisy, 2004, p. 1). The longevity of the Church not only adds a further layer of complexity to this narrative process but also means that it is crucial to address the enduring theological stories.

The challenge this presents is two-fold, in that the Christian story is multi-layered and that in twenty-first-century western culture fewer people seem to be telling it. Sarah Coakley uses Matthew Arnold's metaphor of the sea of faith to describe how theology should address the contemporary world:

> [T]he 'sea of faith' may indeed be murky, polluted, or marshy, existing more in underground streams than in overt ecclesiastical commitment. But its tide is by no means out for ever, and the 'messy entanglement' and detritus that we find in it deserve the closest theological attention. (Coakley, 2013, p. 76)[3]

In other words, theology and the world have to engage with each other and we have to sift through the theological 'detritus' to understand how things stand in the present.

A good example of what happens if the theological narrative is disregarded was provided by the two reports published by the Church of England into leadership at the end of 2014 and the beginning of 2015. The first was entitled *Talent Management for Future Leaders and Leadership Development for Bishops and Deans: A new approach* (popularly known as 'The Green Report'), and the second was called *Senior Church Leadership: A resource for reflection*. *Talent Management* was robustly criticized while *Senior Church Leadership* was more warmly welcomed. There were several reasons for this but, in our view, one of the most important was that the former manifestly failed to engage with the Church's identity stories whereas the latter included two substantial chapters on its organizational autobiography, including its theological and ecclesial narratives. An example of the criticism levelled at *Talent Management* can be found in Martyn Percy's article for *Church Times* in which he argues that 'it has no point of origination in theological or spiritual wisdom. Instead, on offer is a dish of basic contemporary approaches to executive management, with a little theological garnish. A total absence of ecclesiology flows from this' (Percy, 2014).

Understanding the Church as an organization requires an understanding and an account of its theological narrative. In any discussion about leadership and Church/church ministry we need to have a clear sense of what theological stories are being told and how they interact with one another. But these are not the only 'big picture' narratives that shape our perceptions of leadership here, and we have already touched on another key story in the observations of Jeffrey John and Ann Morisy: What kind of ecclesial story is being told by the churches?

What are ecclesial narratives?

One leading writer on organizational storytelling has noted that:

> Stories help communities to pass their spiritual, moral, and cultural heritage from generation to generation . . . In some respects they resemble symbolically endowed artefacts; like symbolic artefacts stories are repositories of meaning, a meaning that both changes and is timeless. Like artefacts, they sustain a set of values and form part of wide networks through which meaning travels. (Gabriel, 2000, p. 88)

And stories in organizations might also have a mythological character (Kostera, 2012), which not only shapes their broader self-understanding, character and values but also impacts upon day-to-day dynamics and decisions. We have already begun to see that in the way that theological and biblical stories affect the self-understanding of churches, and this narrative sense-making process travels through an organization's history.

We noted earlier MacCulloch's (2009) observation about the length of time that the Christian story has been told. This makes for a complex narrative ecology for both the Church and local churches. They are part of much longer narratives which reach back to the development of Christian self-understanding in the

New Testament, and even further back into what Christians call the Old Testament and to theological concepts such as 'the people of God' and 'priesthood' to be found there. These and other metaphors from the ecclesial past continue to shape the organizational sensemaking and storytelling of the Church. Analysing how this process works is part of the task identified by Coakley, which involves working through what she calls the messy entanglements in the sea of faith or, in our terms, the messy ecology of stories.

Thus, for example, ecclesial stories may well include accounts of what took place at the Council of Chalcedon (451), the Great Schism (1054), Luther's publication of his 95 Theses (1517), or the emergence of the Methodist Church (eighteenth century). In his well-reviewed account of Martin Luther's ministry, Scott H. Hendrix argues that Luther's revolutionary innovation was that he defied the established purpose of religion, which was to access the gods and obtain their blessing:

> The exercise of religion required designating holy ground or building temples where sacrifice to the gods could be made; consecrating holy people like priests with power to mediate between believers and the gods, creating sacred rituals and ceremonies to assure the presence of the gods; telling stories about the gods and the world, how it began and how it would end. (Hendrix, 2015, p. 234)

According to Hendrix, Luther sought to change the focus of the ecclesial narrative from one of deeds and external action to one of heart and internal spirituality.

It is striking that the way in which this ecclesial story of reformation is told not only continues to have an impact on how we understand the Church in the present but remains a contested narrative. For instance, Brad S. Gregory's influential analysis of the Reformation is, in essence, a reworking and retelling of this ecclesial story. His narrative is critical of historical accounts that assume progress through distinct periods of culture, or what he calls the 'supersessionist structuring of large scale narratives' (Gregory, 2012, p. 10). Instead, he argues, 'Patterns were established, aspirations justified, expectations naturalized, desires influenced, and new behaviours normalized that need not have taken hold' (p. 11). In other words, as Gabriel has argued, stories are repositories of meaning and one of the ways in which meaning travels through time and culture. The manner in which the ecclesial story of this process is told, from the foundation stories up to the present era, will clearly shape current perceptions of the Church.

The ways in which the theological and ecclesial narratives are enacted will be fundamental to how these stories are understood and their underlying values passed on. And so it is to their retelling in liturgy and worship that we now turn.

What are liturgical narratives?

We mentioned earlier the significance of the Body of Christ as a theological and organizational metaphor for the Church (Carroll) and Martin Luther's attempt to change the ecclesial narrative from one of deeds to one of heart (Hendrix). These two narrative threads are woven together (among others) in what we are calling liturgical narratives. Within Christianity the boundary between divinity and humanity is marked by theology, Church and liturgy. Graham Hughes has particularly explored the liturgical boundary in his volume *Worship as Meaning*. He argues that what he calls the 'narrative configuration' of the liturgy brings together humanity's lived experience with God's transcendent perspective.

For Hughes this moment of worship is set within salvation history or, in our terms, the ecclesial story, and the narrative configuration 'which makes a story out of the actions of the liturgy is the sequence: entrance into, presence within, and return from an encounter with the divine' (Hughes, 2003, pp. 165–6). Thus, liturgy is not just a retelling of a story; it is also about entering into that narrative drama and allowing the encounter in worship to nurture our spiritual lives and dwell in our hearts. As Martin Luther said: 'For where the heart is, everything else is also there' (quoted in Hendrix, 2015, p. 234).

The journalist Andrew Brown and the sociologist of religion Linda Woodhead have given their account of one denomination and its decline through the twentieth century. In *That Was the Church That Was* they argue that religions are complex social constructs and, if you want to understand 'what is happening inside them, you have to observe behaviour and ritual as much as the stories that people tell you about them' (Brown and Woodhead, 2016, p. 68). While we would agree that understanding behaviour and ritual are vitally important, we would argue that they are essential means for retelling a community's story.

In that respect we would see eye to eye with James K. A. Smith who has written extensively about the storied nature of liturgy in the Church and in non-ecclesial culture (Smith, 2009, 2013). He explores how explicit and implicit liturgy shapes our everyday lives and how the Church's worship is closely linked with its organizational storytelling. He writes:

> Liturgies are compressed, repeated, performed narratives that, over time, conscript us into the story they 'tell' by showing, by performing. Such orientating narratives are not explicitly 'told' in a 'once-upon-a-time' discursive mode . . . these stories are more like dramas that are enacted and performed.

In other words, worship carries the Church's 'big Story' and 'we imbibe the Story as we perform in a million little gestures' (Smith, 2013, pp. 109 and 110 – author's capitalization). A key element in this process of liturgical performance and enacted storytelling is the human imagination. As Smith notes: 'Liturgies are those social practices which capture our imaginations by becoming the stories we tell ourselves in order to live' (Smith, 2013, p. 139), and he identifies this as a process working within both sacred and secular cultures.

Sharing interpretive stories

So how do these three stories come together? To conclude this chapter we will analyse a sermon that Vaughan preached at St Mary's Collegiate Church in Warwick as a case study to see how various forms of storytelling can interact during a significant moment of organizational change for a local church. The context was the retirement of one person from a role of significant lay leadership (as one of two churchwardens) and the welcoming of the two people who had been elected to take on this post for the coming year – one of whom had been elected before (Jayne) and one who was new (Clive). This process of marking a change of leadership within the life of one local church was taking place within the context of St Mary's regular choral Eucharist, which itself brings together the theological, ecclesial and liturgical stories we have discussed. In simple terms, the Eucharist or Holy Communion retells the story of Jesus sharing his Last Supper with the disciples and making the symbolic connection between bread/wine and his body/blood. As we have seen, the metaphor of Jesus' body is a fundamental image for the Church and neighbourhood churches, and their organizational narratives, and for many churches the liturgy of communion shapes much of their ongoing performed story.

The sermon preached to mark this important change of leadership in a local church was framed by the theological and biblical narrative of the communal meals that Jesus shared throughout his ministry. Thus, the Gospel passage set for that service was Luke 7.36—8.3, the story of Jesus going to share a meal with one of the religious leaders in his community and then being anointed by a woman whose background the host clearly regarded as dubious. The homily began with the opening sentence of this account, which itself frames that story: 'One of the Pharisees asked Jesus to eat with him, and he went into the Pharisee's house and took his place at table' (Luke 7.36).

Many historians (E. P. Sanders, Dominic Crossan, James D. G. Dunn, N. T. Wright) have regarded these meals in the wider Jewish community as characteristic of Jesus' ministry and as inextricably linked with what is known as Jesus' Last Supper. More recently this view has come in for criticism, and a helpful summary has been provided by Craig Blomberg (2009). After a careful review of the evidence Blomberg concludes there is a strong case for the authenticity of this strand in Jesus' life:

When one inquires about the significance of these meals, one finds repeated hints that Jesus is foreshadowing the eschatological banquet at which he, the key eschatological figure, will partake in a radically inclusive fashion with followers of his from all the people groups on the planet. Indeed, one could speak of these meals as enacted prophecy or symbolic of the kingdom's surprising inclusions. (Blomberg, pp. 61–2)

Having briefly established the theological story Vaughan acknowledges the change of leadership that is taking place: 'This morning we'll be saying thank you to Patrick Wilson for his six years of service as churchwarden and welcoming Jayne McHale and Clive Black as this year's wardens for the Collegiate Church of St Mary.' We can note this as an example of identity narrative (personal story), which we shall explore in Chapter 8.

Vaughan then goes on to say: 'This is a good opportunity to ask: What exactly is a Collegiate Church?' The term 'collegiate church' is unusual in the Church of England and has its origins in the pre-Reformation. As such there are examples across Europe in addition to those found on the British Isles. To all intents and purposes the term exists now mostly as a historical ascription, so a further question naturally occurs – why does it persist? The sermon raises that issue within the context of the broader ecclesial story of collegiate churches: Paul Jeffery's comprehensive book *The Collegiate Churches of England and Wales* (2004) distinguishes seven different types which are briefly outlined.

At this point in the homily we are on the boundary of the ecclesial narrative and what in Chapter 7 we will call the historical narrative. Each local church has its own narrative identity within the story of the Church, and here we can see the story of the 'Collegiate Church of St Mary' emerging from that of the pre- and post-Reformation Church. In Jeffery's terms, St Mary's existed to sing daily masses for its patrons. So, within in the context of changing contemporary leadership, Vaughan asks the congregation to reflect upon the question: In this day and age, what do these roots mean for us now, given that St Mary's principal *raison d'être* – to sing daily masses for dead benefactors – no longer applies? To answer this, he invites his listeners to share in a story told by Fred Craddock, a Professor of Preaching and well-known storyteller based in the USA.

Some years ago there was a new minister who, having finished his training went to serve a little church in what was a small town experiencing massive growth. Everywhere seemed to be a building site; constructors were living in caravans and everyone appeared to be wearing a hard-hat as they laboured to build houses, shops and the other things needed for a growing community. And the new minister's church was close to all this activity. It was a beautiful little church – old and picturesque. It had an organ which one of the youngsters had to pump by hand; it was beautifully decorated and lit by carefully tended paraffin lamps; and every pew in this little church had been hand-carved from trees that had grown near by. This was the place the young minister was going to begin his vocation, his calling from God; and – not long after he'd started – he asked the leaders to stay behind one Sunday and said to them, 'We need to reach out amongst all those caravans and invite those people to church.'

'Oh, I don't know. I don't think they'd fit in,' said one person. 'They're only here temporarily, just construction people,' said another. 'They'll be leaving pretty soon.'

'But we ought to invite them, make them feel at home,' the new minister said. They continued to debate the matter, time ran out and they decided to vote next Sunday. Next Sunday came and everyone sat down after the service. 'I move,' said one person, 'I move that in order to belong to this church you must own property in the town. Someone else said, 'I second that.' The young minister voted against, but the motion passed.

By and by, the young minister was called to serve another church. He got married and raised a family. Eventually he was in the neighbourhood again and he took his wife to see the beautiful old church with the hand-pumped organ, the neat paraffin lamps and . . . the painful memory. It was a challenge but, finally, they found it off a new motorway, down a road, along a gravel track and amongst some pine trees. It was still there but different. There was a car park full of motorbikes, cars and four-wheel drives and a sign saying: All You Can Eat. It was now a restaurant. They went inside. The hand-carved pews were against the wall and there were now electric lights. People were eating at polished tables. 'All kinds of people,' thought the minister, 'Parthians, Medes, Edomites and dwellers of Mesopotamia. Yes . . . All kinds of people.' And the old minister – who'd once been the young minister – said to his wife, 'Well, it's a good thing this isn't still a church, otherwise these people – they couldn't be in here.' (Craddock, 2001, pp. 28–9)

Although it is unacknowledged, it seems clear that the unnamed new minister is the storyteller himself and this account arises directly from his own experience. Furthermore, we can once again detect the three strands of interpretive story at work in Craddock's account. The reference to 'Parthians, Medes, Edomites and dwellers of Mesopotamia' (Acts 2.9) is part of what we are calling the theological story. The young minister's call to evangelism: 'We need to reach out amongst all those caravans and invite those people to church' is a direct link to the ecclesial story and an understanding of the Church as an organization engaged in outreach (perhaps with Matthew 28.19–20 in mind). Meanwhile, the description of 'an organ which one of the youngsters had to pump by hand; it was beautifully decorated and lit by carefully tended paraffin lamps' is part of the performed liturgical story of that church, which the new minister is seeking to change.

Craddock's story works on at least two levels. First, it is about a minister who seeks to lead a community to change the way the congregation tells its ecclesial and liturgical stories, and they refuse. The implied message is: change or die. But there is a second, almost ironic, element to the story in which the kind of people originally excluded from the church building and the hand-carved pews now have access to engage in shared meals – which, as we have seen, are characteristic of Jesus' ministry.

As the sermon draws to a close Vaughan asks the question: What's our vocation as a Collegiate Church in this day and age? And in seeking to provide an answer he contrasts the ecclesial story with the theological story:

We can't go back to pre-Reformation Warwick and continue to sing masses for wealthy benefactors, but we can go back to Jesus of Nazareth and his example of breaking bread, sharing food, with anyone and everyone. It's striking that Jesus never built a church, never wrote a book, never even settled in one place – the Son of Man had nowhere to lay his head. In fact, there's nothing 'solid' about Jesus' ministry and teaching. It was all about relationships – our relationship to God and our relationship to each other – and he described that intricate web of relationships as the Kingdom of God. And this Kingdom was a meal to which everyone was invited – rich and poor, high and low; it was the place where all debts were cancelled; it was the feast where sins were forgiven and healing entered people's lives; it was an encounter at which people would be transformed and life would never be the same again.

Finally, the sermon seeks to draw together its plot lines – including Craddock's story, Jeffery's work on collegiate churches, Jesus' vision for the Kingdom of God and the nature of leadership in the Church/church. In conclusion, Vaughan states that Jesus' teaching is often about relationships, and these make demands of us:

It's much easier to deal with the things that are solid, the things that *don't* change. It's easier to trim the paraffin lamps and polish the pews of the village church than reach out to a community that might be 'here today and gone tomorrow'. And it's striking that, in his detailed description of the Collegiate Church of St Mary's, Warwick, Paul Jeffery spends *one* paragraph talking about the communal element of our life and five paragraphs talking about our building. Now don't get me wrong. This is a wonderful building and it's the most enormous privilege to be the vicar here, and it's part of our Christian stewardship to maintain it; but in the sight of God's Kingdom it's actually much less important than the quality of our relationships – our relationship with God, our relationships with each other and our relationships with the world in which we're set. And churchwardens are an important symbol of this. The office of churchwarden is one of the oldest elected posts in our land and it's a reminder that, as people who're called into God's Kingdom, we're not being called to sing masses for the dead but to proclaim the love of God to the living.

As we have noted, this sermon can be seen as bringing together some of the interpretive stories that we have considered in this chapter, as well as beginning to point ahead to the identity stories we shall examine in Chapter 7. However, at this juncture it is worth pointing out that a sermon itself can be a form of storytelling and story sharing. In particular, it is a type of the 'media' improvised narrative that we shall be discussing in Chapter 8.

This process of weaving narratives together is part of how we create our understanding of reality. Geoff Mead describes it in this way: 'Listening to someone speaking creates the possibility of a unique form of collective experience: we find ourselves coming into a relationship, not just with the speaker and what the speaker is saying, but also with each other' (Mead, 2014, p. 57). It can involve relatively formal approaches to story sharing but it can also be much more informal and unmanaged, among the various forms of improvised storytelling that we shall be considering in due course.

Summary and conclusion

This chapter has explored three forms of interpretive story: (1) Theological narratives; (2) Ecclesial narratives; and (3) Liturgical narratives. We have argued that these stories frame the overall organizational life of the Church in its widest context and in the church in its local forms. We have looked at how theological narratives introduce us to ways in which metaphors function within the Church/church and ways in which both story and metaphor embody issues of power and authority in churches. This is true as well for ecclesial and liturgical narratives. The way in which the various stories of the Church are retold in sermons, guidebooks, websites, books, academic papers, blogs and more, together with the ways in which they are performed and re-enacted in the many different forms of worship and other liturgical activity, all shape communal self-perception and organizational action.

We have illustrated this by exploring how these narrative threads can be woven together in a sermon that one of us preached at a time of significant change of leadership in a church. However, an important caveat needs to be entered here. Human beings tell stories in a particular way. Whether we are talking about someone turning around the fortunes of a school, a company in recovery, changing a church or the response to the Ebola epidemic, we tend to talk about the activities of a few heroic figures. We tell stories, with a hero, a few villains and quite possibly a fool. In David's work he has had the opportunity to talk to a number of those people about whom heroic leadership stories are told. Most of them share a quality of humility, as discussed in Chapter 5, and they want to tell you about the other people who were involved, who were essential to what happened, but who you never read about in the papers. These are the people who did the bits they were bad at, or who were needed because the leadership task was simply too big for one person to carry on their own.

The more we look at the activity of leading in close-up, the less individual it looks. Most activities of any significance are put together by a number of different people exercising different skills. For example, a typical church service of, say, Choral Evensong is put together with a number of different skills, exercised by people with different qualities. Is the service led by the clergy, the musicians, the readers or the person giving the talk? Or even those, long dead, who put together the liturgy or the building? On a good day, the answer is that parts of it are led by different people working together to bring about something special, each feeling released to step forward to lead at some points and, equally importantly, stepping back to enable others to lead at other points.

The same is true about the process of storytelling and story sharing. As we have seen in this chapter, these are sensemaking activities which require collective participation, because one sermon by one person in a local church is not the beginning and end of leadership. We shall go on to explore other aspects of this approach as we turn in the following chapter to examine the nature of identity stories.

Questions

1 What kinds of interpretive story are being told in the church communities of which you are a part?

2 Who is telling those stories? Whose stories are the most powerful and why?

3 What is happening when different interpretive stories are being told and how are conflicting narratives resolved?

Notes

1 See Roberts 2017 for discussion of other typologies of the Church.

2 Aired on 10 April 2016, available at www.youtube.com/watch?v=JGmM2yaNdNg (from 1 minute 40 seconds), accessed 12.9.2016.

3 Vaughan has used R. S. Thomas' poem 'Tidal' to address the same issue (Roberts 1997), and has explored in detail how water can function as a metaphor in churches for organizational change (Roberts 2002a) and as an image for organizational storytelling.

7

Church Narratives: Identity Stories

Introduction

In the previous chapter we explored three forms of story that frame a wider understanding of the Church's ministry – theological, ecclesial and liturgical narratives. This chapter examines another three manifestations of story which shape more local perceptions of Church and churches. We are calling these identity stories because they describe how churches and individuals within churches discern their self-understanding. In particular, we have identified (1) Historical narratives, (2) Organizational narratives, and (3) Personal narratives (see Figure 2); and all three involve 'thick' descriptions of what they are depicting. For instance, the historical heading involves not only the story of each local church but also the national and social context in which it is set.

A simple illustration of this comes from the Anglican service of Evensong which is said and sung by churches of the same denomination in England, the United States and across the Anglican Communion. However, there are some significant local variations. For example, there is a set response which in one country is rendered 'O Lord, save the Queen' (England) and in another 'O Lord, save the state' (USA). That small alteration of a simple five-letter word not only points to a bitter war of independence but also hints at the enormous social and intellectual transformations wrought through the changes of the western Enlightenment.

The same is true of the other two narrative headings. The ways we understand those organizations in which we work and those

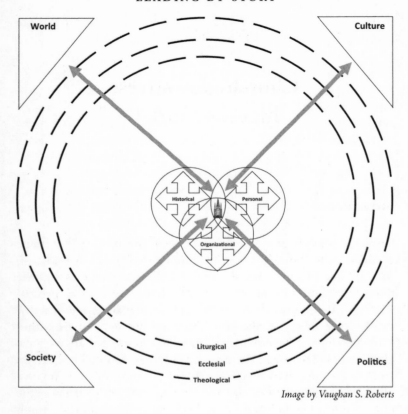

Image by Vaughan S. Roberts

Figure 2: Identity Stories.

that impact upon our lives will vary enormously, and the ways in which they are led and managed, how they strategize and engage in the process of sensemaking will be complex and multi-layered – as will the stories told about all of those processes. Many of those stories will involve characters who have stood out or people who have been important at a more personal level. And what about the person telling the story? As Gabriel notes:

Story is a poetic elaboration on events, one that accords with the needs of the teller and the audience, and one that requires considerable ingenuity on the part of the narrator. Storytellers must walk the tricky tightrope across two potentially undermining questions – the 'so what?' question and the 'did it really?' question. (Gabriel, 2004, p. 20)[1]

We must keep those questions in mind as we listen, hear and read the stories that are being offered to us because, if nothing else, the narrators' identity stories will be shaping their telling of all the other stories.

We have developed our initial diagram from Chapter 6 to place the historical, organizational and personal stories in close proximity to the church, and these identity stories continue to be framed by the interpretive stories we outlined there. But this inner core of narrative identity will also affect the broader, interpretive narratives. For instance, as we have already noted, both of us were involved for a time in the ministry of Christ Church, Bath – a Church of England proprietary chapel. Such chapels are historical anomalies in the Church of England and, to understand and lead its ministry, it was important to know the historical story of why they were created and their unusual position within the current church structures.

An important aspect of that church's self-understanding was its self-description of having a 'people's ministry' and how the organizational metaphor of 'people' was functioning in that context, along with additional images that were being employed in the organizational story. Another key element in the story at that time was the presence of the longest-serving archdeacon in the Church of England who was keen to resolve the anomalous status of Christ Church as one of his final acts before retirement. Thus all three stories – historical, organizational and personal – were in play as that church sought to write the next chapter of its organizational autobiography at that time.

Identity stories are essentially about 'who we are and where we are going' (Mead, 2014, p. 149), and a number of writers speak of organizations as having an autobiography. For example, Monika Kostera argues: 'An organizational autobiography is a story that is continuous, yet unfinished – as long as the organization is in existence, it is retold and often reinterpreted' (Kostera, 2012, p. 49). And, as Wheatley contends, a key leadership role is defining identity: '[O]ne of the primary tasks of a leader is to make sure the organization knows itself . . . When this clear identity is available, it serves every member of the organization' (Wheatley, 2006, p. 169).

Of course identity stories are not confined to organizations, since individuals tell their own personal stories in relation to and separately from those groups for whom they work or with whom they have a formal connection. It is clear that within the context of organizational storytelling individuals explore, try out and develop different identities for themselves (Gabriel, 2000, p. 129). So let us examine each form of identity story more closely.

What are historical narratives?

We have already touched upon this in our reference to Christ Church as a proprietary chapel, but each local church will have its own story that develops through time. In his reference to Paul Ricoeur's extensive work on time and narrative, Geoff Mead comments:

> The relationship between time and narrative is a fascinating and rewarding subject for philosophical study, but for our purposes the essential point is that telling stories is how we make sense of experience in relation to the passage of time – past, present and future. (Mead, 2014, p. 219)

A fascinating recent example is the Cathedral Church of St Martin in Leicester. The historical narrative on its website tells us that the Diocese of Leicester was established in AD 680 but that after 200 years their bishop fled in the face of Viking invasion.[2] The diocese was re-established in 1927 and St Martin's church, which had been started by the Normans and enlarged over the centuries, became its cathedral. In recent years the surrounding area has been redeveloped as a local school moved to new premises and the diocese and cathedral bought that property. That process began a significant new chapter in the cathedral's story which was extended again when the body of Richard III was discovered near by and re-interred in the cathedral.

One of us was privileged to walk around the area with the Dean, David Monteith, and see the king's tomb and the simultaneous reordering of the cathedral with the building of the city's Richard

III Visitor Centre near by. It was also striking to hear the Dean talk about the changed perceptions of Leicester Cathedral brought about by this new stage in the story of Richard III. It was a good example of how a national story, a local story and the story of one church can interact through past, present and future. The evolution of the cathedral square will continue, since another building has been recently purchased opposite the cathedral and will be developed in due course.

Another instance from regular parish ministry is provided by the narrative review undertaken by the six churches in the Warwick Team. Vaughan has written about this elsewhere (Roberts, 2014), but one thing that emerged from listening to the congregations' historical stories was how completely different they were even within what, on the surface, was one denomination in the same town. For example, St Mary's is a large historic church in the centre of Warwick and part of its historic story is linked to the great fire of Warwick (1694). Although the conflagration did not reach as far as the church, locals took shelter in the building with their remaining belongings. Some of these were still smouldering, caught fire and burnt down the nave, which was subsequently rebuilt in a different architectural style. For some, this historical story of open doors at great cost to the church remains an important part of the contemporary narrative of a ministry of welcome.

By contrast, St Paul's church is a smaller, local church barely five minutes' walk from St Mary's. It was established as the servants' church for those worshipping at the large civic building. At the time of undertaking the ministerial review, St Paul's was able to integrate this element of their historical narrative and tell their own identity story as one of being the 'serving church'. At the other end of Warwick, All Saints, Emscote is a modern church building constructed in the 1980s after the Victorian church was demolished for safety reasons in the 1960s. However, the team vicar at All Saints at the time of the review reported that there were still parishioners who would not attend church because a previous vicar and the diocesan authorities had had the original church building demolished on the 'pretence' of architectural problems. Each of the other three congregations (Christchurch, St Michael's and St Nicholas) had their own distinctive historical narrative, which shape their contemporary improvised stories that we shall explore further in Chapter 8.

As cathedrals and churches continue to tell their stories, they weave together elements of the past, present and future. Such organizational narratives will include the story of the building itself as well as aspects of the wider historical and social story. They will not necessarily include the reburial of a dead monarch or the rediscovery of a foundation document but there will still be characters and components from past stories that will continue to shape and influence that organizational story in the present and the future.

What are organizational narratives?

The language that any organization uses about itself is clearly going to be significant and will reflect its self-understanding. Often this will employ metaphorical language as we noted in Chapter 6 with Jackson W. Carroll's discussion of how salt, light, household, clay jars, people of God and royal priesthood shape understandings of leadership in churches. In our approach, we follow Lakoff and Johnson in arguing for the fundamentally metaphorical nature of language (Lakoff and Johnson, 1980; Lakoff, 1987; Johnson, 1987).

There has been widespread analysis of metaphor across the range of organizational behaviour, for example in management (Morgan, 1997), strategy (Mintzberg, Ahlstrand and Lampel, 1998), and leadership (Alvesson and Spicer, 2011). Thus, Morgan notes:

> Metaphor is often regarded just as a device for embellishing discourse but its significance is much greater than this. The use of metaphor implies *a way of thinking* and *a way of seeing* that pervade how we understand our world generally. (Morgan, 1997, p. 4 – author's italics)

Alvesson and Spicer draw attention to the importance of metaphor and vocabulary for leadership: '[T]he language that we use to describe leadership shapes what exactly we can understand as being leadership. Leadership here is both a matter of the overall framing and the specific use of vocabulary in specific settings' (Alvesson and Spicer, 2011, p. 45).

One strong and recurring metaphor which continues to have an impact on how churches perceive their ministry is that of the 'sea of faith'. It comes from Matthew Arnold's poem 'Dover Beach' (published in 1867) and, in particular, that part of the third stanza which reads:

The Sea of Faith
Was once, too, at the full, and round earth's shore
Lay like the folds of a bright girdle furl'd.
But now I only hear
Its melancholy, long, withdrawing roar,
Retreating, to the breath
Of the night-wind, down the vast edges drear
And naked shingles of the world.

This has long been taken as a metaphor for the receding nature of religion in western culture: good examples can be found in the work of Nicholas Lash and Don Cupitt. Lash acknowledged, in his inaugural lecture as Norris-Hulse Professor of Divinity in the University of Cambridge, that the task of a Christian theologian was now critical because '[t]he sea has retreated too far down Dover beach for it to be otherwise' (Lash, 1979, p. 5). And as Cupitt rightly observes in his book that takes Arnold's image as its title: 'The sea of faith, in Matthew Arnold's great metaphor, flows as well as ebbs; but the tide that returns is not quite the same as the tide that went out' (Cupitt, 1988, p. 18). This image has been revisited by Sarah Coakley who has contrasted Dover Beach with Wigan Pier, arguing that some theologians have sought to rise above the messy entanglements and detritus of the tidal beach by creating a theology that (like Wigan Pier) is cut off from the sea, which may be murky and polluted (Coakley, 2013, p. 76).[3]

Our aim at this point is not to seek some kind of resolution for this metaphor, because, as Cupitt notes, the tide will continue to ebb and flow. Indeed, we can place this image alongside Gareth Morgan's metaphor of organization as flux and change (Morgan,

1997) which uses streams, whirlpools and other fluid ideas to describe organizational change. The key question is: What impact does such imagery have upon the accounts of a church's ministry? For instance, the story being told by a church that feels the tide of faith is fast receding will probably be different from that which feels the sea is all around it, with consequences that we discussed in Chapter 3, and will elaborate on further in Chapter 9. Similarly a church built well above the swirl of changing social and theological beliefs (on Wigan Pier) will be sharing a different organizational narrative with those inside and outside that ecclesial community.

There are numerous metaphorical descriptions of the Church. One of the most influential has been provided by Avery Dulles SJ. His original work set out five models of the Church: Institution, Mystical Communion, Sacrament, Herald and Servant; his updated edition added the model of School of Discipleship (Dulles, 1987). Other ways of modelling churches have been proposed since Dulles (for example Morisy, 2004; Billings, 2010; Cameron, 2010). This variety of language, image and metaphor is crucial to the storytelling process. An organizational story that sees a group's behaviour as organic will be different from that where the workplace is perceived as a situation of domination or power (Morgan, 1997).

People in positions of leadership will tell different stories if they see their roles as creating clear direction or making people feel good (Alvesson and Spicer, 2011). In a conversation one of us had with a cathedral dean, she described clergy as 'pirates' and spoke of how they hoist up the Jolly Roger, set sail in their boats and are responsible to no one but themselves. By contrast, she argued, cathedrals teach us to be responsible to the wider Church and community, and to work together as a team. Experienced sailors would undoubtedly argue that sailing a large boat necessarily involves teamwork, and experienced priests would probably argue the same applies to parish ministry; but this metaphor asks us to reflect upon the place and role of teamwork in churches both large and small. Here we have a sense of how organizational metaphor has great power but also needs to be treated with critical attention, and we can see this more clearly by exploring a children's story about a rabbit.

Both authors discovered Margery Williams' story *The Velveteen Rabbit* long after our childhoods. Vaughan cannot remember when he was first introduced to it – he thinks it was through an anthology of Easter readings, although he cannot remember which one. But David has a clear recollection of hearing it on his car radio. We have both found it helpful in our professional lives – Vaughan has used it in sermons and David has used it to reflect upon the nature of organizations. In his piece entitled 'The velveteen rabbit and passionate feelings for organizations' David expresses a sense of being perplexed as 'years of theoretical thinking were undermined by a rabbit' (Sims, 2004, p. 209).

In essence the story is about a toy rabbit who, over time, becomes a child's favourite toy. The boy loved his velveteen rabbit and the rabbit himself was very happy – so happy, in fact, that he didn't notice that his velveteen fur was getting shabbier and shabbier; his tail was coming unsewn; and all the pink had been rubbed off his nose. But it didn't matter because they were both happy . . . One day the boy took the velveteen rabbit off to play in a nearby wood and the rabbit found himself left alone for a while in the grass. Along came some curious creatures. They seemed to be rabbits like himself but quite furry and brand-new. They must have been very well made, for their seams didn't show and they changed shape as they moved along. One minute they were long and thin, whilst the next they were fat and bunchy. As he talked to these rabbits, the velveteen rabbit began to realize there were things which these rabbits could do and he couldn't – he always thought he was real, but now things weren't so clear.

At one point there's a conversation between the velveteen rabbit and his friend, the toy horse, which explores this realization. 'What is real?' asked the Rabbit one day, when they were lying side by side. 'Does it mean having things that buzz inside you and a stick out handle?'

'Real isn't how you are made,' said the Rocking Horse. 'It's a thing that happens to you. When a child loves you for a long, long time, not just to play with but really loves you, then you become real.'

'Does it hurt?' asked the Rabbit.

'Sometimes,' said the Rocking Horse. 'You become. It takes a long time. That's why it doesn't often happen to people who break easily, or who have sharp edges, or who have to be carefully kept. Generally, by the time you are real, most of your hair has been loved off, and your eyes drop out and you get loose in the joints and very shabby. But these things don't matter at all, because once you are real you can't be ugly, except to people who don't understand. And the rabbit is loved into life by the boy.'

David notes how much contemporary analysis of organizations resists the idea of personifying corporations, charities and other institutions. Yet the idea of treating them as more like persons has a long history, as evidenced by Paul's use of the body as a metaphor for the Church in 1 Corinthians 12.12–16. By describing a number of examples from schools, a small business, a university department and a professional body David explores the impact that love does or does not have upon an institution. For example, the biggest problem for the professional body was that 'plenty of people are prepared to devote a little time and energy to it, but no one loves it sufficiently for it to come to life. It remains doggedly velveteen; it never quite gets loved to life' (Sims, 2004, p. 216).

Here we can see organizational narrative and organizational metaphor coming together. Gabriel observes how metaphors are one of a number of 'devices in the storyteller's armour' (Gabriel, 2000, p. 35). Organizational meaning is generated through participants' (leaders' *and* followers') use of all kinds of poetic tropes in the telling and retelling of a church's story. The metaphors we choose for our stories in churches are fundamental to how the processes of sensemaking work out. The language that leaders use about followers and the language used by followers about leaders will be an integral part of how organizational narratives are recounted and whether a church (or any other organization, for that matter) ever gets loved into life.

This process of choosing metaphors and telling stories happens within a historical context and within organizations but they also involve individuals and people's own personal narratives. In his book *The Leader's Guide to Storytelling* Stephen Denning notes:

> Each of us ends up making a unique set of choices or nonchoices that reflect the course of action that we take or don't take, and embodies those choices in a personal story . . . Whether explicit or emergent, there is always a life story of some kind. (Denning, 2011b, pp. 98–9)

It is to those personal narratives that we now turn.

What are personal narratives?

Personal stories come in many forms so we shall refer briefly to two under this heading: (1) one's own story; and (2) other key personal stories in the church. Geoff Mead argues that stories are 'the primary way we make sense of our experience, giving meaning and significance to our lives and creating (and re-creating) our sense of self', as well as being 'a vital means of building relationships, bringing groups and communities together (discounting others' stories can cause conflict and divisions)' (Mead, 2014, p. 18). In other words, people's personal stories can play an important role within an organizational context, as can the stories of those around us and the stories of past actors in the organizational drama.

A healthy church will find ways of weaving these stories together. Writing from a theological perspective William Dyrness observes:

> Our lives (and our cultures) are a complex arrangement of many little stories. Some of them – the way we select our clothes, arrange our furniture, or set the table for guests – have specific aesthetic purposes. But I would argue that all of them, in some sense, serve aesthetic and religious purposes. How is this so? It is because our projects are constructed with a view to our enjoyment, but beyond this, because they are, ultimately, shaped to praise or honor what we think is important. (Dyrness, 2011, p. 77)

Churches often bring together a contrasting array of little stories, including the autobiographical narratives of those *presently* working there (such as clergy, volunteers, vergers) and those who use the buildings (for instance, worshippers, tourists, local stakeholders), but also the biographies of *previous* clergy, past bell ringers, even former animals or pets. During the writing of this book one of us visited some churches in the USA including the Cathedral of St John the Divine, New York, and came across a small but typical example. In that vast building the symbol for the Anglican Communion, the compass rose, is set into the floor (see Figure 3). It was designed by a venerable priest of the cathedral, Canon Edward West, who is now buried beneath it. In conversation the Canon Precentor remarked how she would instruct processions to turn right at the compass rose, while longstanding members of the serving team would *relay* that instruction in the form of: 'Turn right at Canon West.'

That is an example of a key personal story in church and most local churches encourage this form of narrative. Frequently there will be a board with the names of previous vicars and ministers, or there may be a section of the church where pictures of past clergy are displayed. But what about one's own story?

Again in the USA we heard a good example of using one's personal narrative to establish rapport with a congregation. Andreas Loewe was born in Germany, trained for ordained ministry in England and was serving as Dean of Melbourne Cathedral in Australia. He was

Photograph by Vaughan S. Roberts

Figure 3: Compass Rose in the Cathedral of St John the Divine, New York.

visiting the National Cathedral in Washington yet in his sermon was able to locate his personal story alongside that of the congregation he was addressing:

> Although I have come a long way today, I am not a complete stranger to your neighbourhood: some eighteen years ago, I had the privilege of living in Cathedral Heights. Then, I was a seminarian from the Church of England working at an inner-city parish in your diocese, and I daily undertook the audacious (some might say foolhardy) commute by bike from my temporary home near your beautiful Cathedral down to the centre of town via Wisconsin Avenue and Dumbarton Oaks. The way to work was exhilarating and fast; the way home was quite literally an uphill struggle. (Loewe, 17 May 2015)[4]

He went on to speak about vocational journeys but in that narrative opening we have an example of someone's personal story being entwined with the historical and organizational story of a specific place, which then connects to the wider story of theological identity. This is only part of the narrative complexity in personal stories. The aspects of personal narrative in that sermon will only have been part of a much richer, autobiographical account distributed over various different characteristics, interests and events (Sims, 2005). As one writer on leadership has succinctly put it: 'Your story changes and you appropriate the things that make you who you are' (Ibarra, 2015, p. 154), and that sense of who we are will develop over time and change according to our context.

One way of exploring that change of story according to context is provided by Simon P. Walker, who has taken the metaphor of front and back stage from the theatre, and applied that to his ideas and experience of personal leadership (Walker, 2011). In particular, he examines how different forms of ego practise different approaches to leadership. He argues that undefended forms of leadership are much more healthy for all forms of organization but there are a number of different types of ego so our different characters need to cultivate this approach in different ways. Thus, he identifies (1) the Defining Ego, which is over-confident, yet fears failure; (2) the Shaping Ego, which takes responsibility but disempowers others; (3) the Adapting Ego, which lacks self-trust and fears to say 'no'; (4) the Defending Ego, which shows a lack of trust in others and a fear of risk (Walker, 2011, pp. 132–7).

The key aspect of this for us is not whether we agree with Walker's analysis and precise definitions of ego, but the importance of different characters and how they respond to the challenges of leadership. We have touched on the range of leadership metaphors available in organizations (Alvesson and Spicer, 2011) and in churches (Hybels, 2002; Lamdin, 2012). The way in which those involved in leading congregations will choose metaphors and tell stories will undoubtedly be shaped by their characters and their self-understanding. To understand why someone is recounting the *organizational* story that they are telling will necessarily require understanding their *personal* story as well.

Sharing identity stories?

Given these three forms of identity story, how do they interact? A good illustration of how this works was provided at Birmingham Cathedral, which one of us visited on its patronal festival, which was celebrating the cathedral's three hundredth anniversary. The preacher was David Ford, Lay Canon at Birmingham and at the time Regius Professor of Divinity at the University of Cambridge, who was speaking on Isaiah 30.15–21, Ephesians 1.3–10 and John 14.1–14.[5] His sermon provides helpful illustrations of how the process of identity and interpretive storytelling works. He begins by making a direct connection between the interpretive stories outlined in Chapter 6 and two identity stories (historical and personal) at the centre of our model of organizational narrative (see Figure 2 on page 108).

Thus he began his sermon by saying:

It is a great delight to be here with you today to celebrate the patronal festival of this Cathedral in its tercentenary year. For 15 of those 300 years I lived here in inner city Birmingham, and I developed not only a love for this wonderful city but also a great respect for the way this diocese has combined following Jesus Christ and serving the welfare of the city and the region.

Those two sentences immediately link the story of the cathedral and his personal story with the historical narrative of Jesus and the theological narrative of Jesus' messiahship. Ford strengthens all of those connections when he continues: 'In our fascinating readings from scripture today the orientation and horizon for what this cathedral church is about is set by the glorious first chapter of the letter to the Ephesians.'

The sermon goes on to make a connection between the interpretive narratives of theology and liturgy, while explicitly placing the present life of the cathedral and city within the circle of the Christian theological story:

> [T]he first priority is what we are doing here this morning, blessing God, praising God, thanking God, affirming that this cathedral is here thanks to God, that this city is here thanks to God, and that the basic motivation for all we do is that we do it for God's sake.

David Ford also places the whole of creation within that story, which

> includes all people, all religions, all cultures, all academic disciplines, all industries, all areas of life and society, all parts of ourselves. God is committed to all that in love and compassion, and so, therefore, are we called to be too.

Then he turns to the challenging statement from the Gospel reading where Jesus says, 'I am the way, and the truth, and the life. No one comes to the Father except through me.' Ford argues that this means that Jesus is already in relationship with all people, all religions, all creation, just as God is. This open relationship to creation is modelled by Jesus when he takes the role of a slave to wash his disciples' feet. Ford once again uses the theological narrative to shape what we are calling churches' improvised stories when he asks: 'What would Birmingham Cathedral look like in its fourth century if it imaginatively developed more ministries that had the DNA of Jesus' action in washing feet?'

He concludes by returning to his own personal story, specifically his experience of sharing in the practice of Scriptural

Reasoning where Jews, Christians, Muslims and other traditions have come together to read and dissect passages from their scriptures. He describes this as a process of deepening which involves: 'going deeper into my own scriptures, deeper into those of other traditions, deeper into our commitment to the common good of our world beyond our own communities, deeper into our disagreements as well as our agreements'. That aspect of his own story has led him to reflect further on the Christian theological and ecclesial narratives – in particular, Jesus' saying, 'In my Father's house there are many dwelling places.' Ford concludes: 'That house sounds rather like a pluralist place. What surprises may be in store for us as we go from dwelling-place to dwelling-place meeting other members of the family to whom God is our Father?'

Although David Ford does not use the terms 'story' or 'narrative' in this sermon, we would contend that his homily provides good examples of how the interpretive stories located in theology, ecclesiology and liturgy shape the space for, and interact with, the improvised and identity stories of the Church and churches.

Summary and conclusion

This chapter has explored three forms of identity story: (1) Historical narratives; (2) Organizational narratives; and (3) Personal narratives. We have argued that the way in which these stories are told will fashion the sensemaking of local churches, from small communities to large cathedrals. Each church has a unique history and the story (or stories) that are told about its past shape its self-understanding of the present and its expectations for the future. As we saw with the churches in Warwick, the story of the servants' church will be qualitatively and spiritually different from the church that has had its building replaced in controversial circumstances.

The metaphors that congregations use in talking about their ministry and mission will also form and inform the construction of their narratives. If clergy are seen as pirates setting sail to plunder or loot then the kind of stories told will be very different from those where clergy themselves are seen as a form of servant

(Dulles, 1987) or as rabbits seeking to love or be loved (Sims, 2004). However, as Walker notes, even servants come in various forms and will give different accounts of how they see that ministry and those of the churches they lead (Walker, 2011).

Anthony de Mello was a Indian Jesuit priest and writer on spirituality. He was also a great collector and teller of stories. In one he imagines Jesus going to a game of American football and an interaction within the crowd:

> Jesus Christ said he had never been to a football match. So we took him to one, my friends and I. It was a ferocious battle between the Protestant Punchers and the Catholic Crusaders. The Crusaders scored first. Jesus cheered wildly and threw his hat high up in the air. Then the Punchers scored. And Jesus cheered wildly and threw his hat high up in the air.
>
> This seemed to puzzle the man behind us. He tapped Jesus on the shoulder and asked, 'Which side are you rooting for, my good man?'
>
> 'Me?' replied Jesus, visibly excited by the game. 'Oh, I'm not rooting for either side. I'm just enjoying the game.'
>
> The questioner turned to his neighbour and sneered, 'Hmm, an atheist!' (de Mello, 1984, pp. 147–8)

That parable is about identity and references the three identity stories that we have discussed in this chapter. To appreciate the plot we need to know something about the historical story of Protestant and Catholic forms of Christianity and how they have continued to manifest themselves in sport. Thus, in the UK the same story could be told about matches between Liverpool and Everton or Rangers and Celtic. At the same time, it is also an organizational fable. Yes, it is a story about a football match but it is a story about different manifestations of communal faith as well. On the face of it, the story is about football teams but it works because it is also about the Church and about alternative perspectives on faith. Finally, it is a personal narrative, which is not just about an individual taking Jesus to a football match with a group of friends – in itself, an interesting storytelling device – but also asks listeners to reflect upon their own positions on faith. Are they a supporter? Are they someone who judges others? Do they just enjoy the game? Are they an atheist? And, wherever they see themselves, how do they assess the action of each person in the narrative?

In Chapter 6 we explored some of the dynamics around the 'big picture' stories of the Church, its theology and Scripture, and its liturgy, all of which function as interpretive stories. In this chapter we have begun to examine some of the key identity narratives and how an understanding of a church's history can shape storytelling alongside organizational perceptions and personal stories of those involved with churches. In the next chapter we shall see how these interpretive and identity narratives shape the space for the every-day sharing and telling of churches' improvised stories.

Questions

1 What have been the essential historical narratives of the churches that you have belonged to and how were they different from one another?
2 Which metaphors are important to you in describing the Church and can you see how they shape your own sensemaking?
3 Have you been in churches where a past personal story has continued to fashion the current narrative, and how has your personal story fitted into that situation?

Notes

1 Ibarra makes a similar point: 'Seldom is a good story so needed as when we want others to believe what we believe so that they will act as we want them to act' (Ibarra, 2015, p. 64).

2 http://leicestercathedral.org/about-us/history-of-leicester-cathedral/, accessed 30.3.2017.

3 Andrew Brown and Linda Woodhead also continue to use this image in their account of the 'disappearance' of the Church of England (Brown and Woodhead, 2016).

4 The full text can be found here: https://cathedral.org/sermons/page /11/, accessed 30.3.2017.

5 Professor Ford's sermon can be found here on Birmingham Cathedral's website: www.birminghamcathedral.com/recentevents/, accessed 30.3.2017.

8

Church Narratives:
Improvised Stories

Introduction

In her insightful analysis of leadership Donna Ladkin observes that meaning is 'iterative and emergent' (Ladkin, 2010, p. 112) and that organizational meaning-making is a 'jointly negotiated activity' (p. 114). Living stories play a vital role in this process of negotiation. Furthermore, as Kostera notes, such stories 'leave space for improvisation and adjustment to context. They are an ideal method of sense-making in contemporary organizations' (Kostera, 2012, p. 22). She draws attention to how such narrative is used to manage information in organizations characterized by pace of action and complexity of structure. There are times when the pace of life in churches and cathedrals can be relatively calm but at other times it is frenetic. Against this backdrop of activity all forms of church life have some form of governance structure which provides a framework for their everyday and improvised stories.

In terms of the ecology of church narrative that we are mapping out, this part is the most complex and diverse. These are the stories being cultivated or improvised in local churches which – depending upon specific climate and conditions – can grow in a wide variety of different ways. However, whatever the governance structures in place, recent organizational theory has suggested that we need to work on the 'Red Queen principle', based on Lewis Carroll's Red Queen who says that 'in this place it takes all the running you can do, to keep in the same place'. Gustafsson and Lindahl (2015) say that this principle makes improvised and intuitive action and decision-making not a shortcoming in organizational life, but an essential. We shall consider nine areas of improvised narrative, though that does not preclude the emergence of other species or sub-genres.

The metaphor of improvisation was used in the report *Senior Church Leadership* (see page 94), which has been reprinted under the title *Faithful Improvisation: Theological Reflections on Church Leadership*. Paragraph 119 states:

> The New Testament church does not provide us with a single model of leadership. Instead, it provides us with a fluid picture of ongoing adaptation, in which the divisions of ministry tasks between people and leaders, and between local and trans-local leaders, were re-negotiated in the light of changing circumstances and developing understanding, as was the nature of the task itself. That negotiation took place between what Christians in any particular local context were *given*, and what they *found*. They sought to do justice to these different situations (*locality*) while remaining recognizable to those in other locales (*catholicity*) and faithful to what they had inherited (*apostolicity*) – and that required of them creative and flexible improvisation. (§119, *Senior Church Leadership*, p. 48; *Faithful Improvisation*, p. 53 – our italics)

The original report and the subsequent reflective commentary do not provide any detailed analysis of how this image of improvisation is being employed or the implications of its use. In organizational theory it tends to be linked either to a musical or a theatrical context. Thus, Fineman, Sims and Gabriel note that there 'has been considerable recent interest in improvisation as a way of understanding actions in organizations'.

> Like the jazz player, the skilled operator in a meeting does not know exactly how his or her performance is going to turn out beforehand. It will depend on how the other performers are behaving, on the mood of the moment, and on good ideas which occur at the time. Improvisation thus becomes a much more convincing metaphor for actions in organizations than any more scripted notion that implies more detailed planning. (Fineman, Sims and Gabriel, 2005, p. 351)

The metaphor of jazz as a means of describing organizational complexity is touched upon by Tim Harle in his response to *Faithful Improvisation*, along with that of bricolage, but they are not explored in detail (Harle, 2016, p. 206).

By contrast Mangham and Overington in their application of a theatrical metaphor to understanding organizational dynamics observe:

> Performances are always open to improvisation, to disruption, to success and failure, to change; they are open to considerations of actors and their characters, to settings and their expression; they are open to the nature and conduct of audiences. Textuality, as a particular sense about performances, exists precisely *as a result* of performance. (Mangham and Overington, 1987, p. 199 – authors' italics)

As we noted in Chapter 7 Simon Walker also uses theatre and narrative as images for understanding how organizations and leadership work. He describes the leader as

> a director who creates a piece of theatre in which she invites her followers to play their parts. She needs to be the one who draws the 'story arc' of the whole community. She may leave it to her cast to develop the script themselves, but she herself takes responsibility for the trajectory of the story. (Walker, 2011, p. 318)

Although Walker does not use the word 'improvisation' it is implied in the potential for the cast to develop their script.

So by improvised stories we mean those scripts that are presently under development and being negotiated to be performed within the life of churches and cathedrals. This chapter has been informed by field work that Vaughan undertook on a period of sabbatical study leave, exploring storytelling within Anglican cathedrals in the UK and USA. Cathedrals tend to be larger churches both physically and numerically, often with a particular civic and tourist ministry – although, inevitably, within Anglicanism there are exceptions to this. While this part of the narrative ecology draws upon the analysis Vaughan undertook in cathedrals, we have also mapped it on to our own experience in a variety of much smaller and more local congregations and believe these improvised stories can be found throughout most parts of the ecclesial garden. Those narratives that we will be exploring are: (1) Finance, (2) Architecture, (3) Governance, (4) Pastoral, (5) Mission, (6) Education, (7) Media, (8) Art, all of which, we believe, apply in one form or another to most churches (see Figure 4). And there is one further narrative form ('Untended stories') that will be considered in due course under this heading.

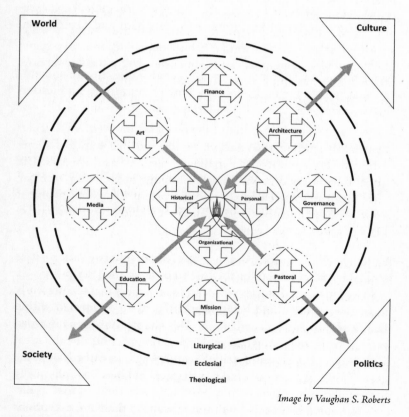

Image by Vaughan S. Roberts

Figure 4: Improvised Stories.

Finance

Under improvised stories we shall begin with finance, since in our experience it is striking how prominently money and the funding of ministry have featured in all the churches with which we have been involved. This was also the case in the conversations that Vaughan undertook with serving deans in both the UK and the USA in preparation for this book: commercial challenges were a prominent feature of their ministries.

It might seem counter-intuitive to see finance as a story – surely this is about figures and numbers rather than story and narrative? Interestingly, in a public lecture the mathematician and Simonyi Professor for the Public Understanding of Science at the University of Oxford, Marcus du Sautoy, makes the case that mathematics is a form of narrative.[1] He argues: 'Mathematicians are storytellers. Our characters are numbers and geometries. Our narratives are the proofs we create about these characters' (10 minutes 30–41 seconds). Speaking of Fermat's Last Theorem, du Sautoy says:

> It is the narrative character of the proof of this theorem that elevates this true statement about numbers to the status of something deserving of its place in the pantheon of mathematics. The quality of a good proof has many things in common with the act of great storytelling. My conjecture, if I'm going to put it into terms of a mathematical equation, is that proof = narrative. (11 minutes 14–54 seconds)[2]

For those who still have reservations about the common ground between narrative and mathematics, it remains the case that the fiscal wellbeing of a church provides the basis for much of its organizational activity and storytelling. While finance continues to be figures, when someone is competent at finance they know how to tell a story from those figures.

A good example can be found in the Dean's introduction to the 2015/16 Programme for Salisbury Cathedral. June Osborne writes:

> As we embark on this Programme we give thanks for all those who have made possible the removal of scaffolding on the

North side of the Cathedral . . . a sight not seen for many years. We are also grateful to those who made possible the installation of the new Magna Carta exhibition in the Chapter House and Cloisters, alongside the wide-ranging programme of events and learning programmes . . . While there is still much to be done to complete the Major Repair Programme, now is the time to start to look beyond repair and to plan for our future challenges. This programme is designed to do just that; we are investing in the future. (p. 3)[3]

We can see how Osborne is framing the current challenges in terms of the ongoing story of the cathedral (in this instance, the historic removal of scaffolding from the north side and the even longer-term narrative of Magna Carta), while at the same time describing all of this with the financial metaphor of 'investing in the future'.

Significantly, in his chapter on narratives and transmitting values Stephen Denning recounts a story told by someone who borrowed some money from his family:

Just after I got out of the college, I wanted to start a business, and I needed to borrow $500. My parents wouldn't lend it to me. So I went to Uncle Ben and explained what I was going to do and he lent me $500. And then the business foundered and the money was gone. The business was gone and I owed Uncle Ben this money. I didn't call him back. I just kind of severed the relationship. That's how I felt. After 6 months of no payment, he called me. I remember he said: 'You know, you just don't do this. This is not the way to treat someone who trusted you. It's OK that you don't have the money. We can work out a way for you to get the money and pay it back over time. But it's not okay to break off the relationship like that.' And that stayed with me for my whole life, how one manages money, how one deals with people who have trusted you. (Seth Kahan in Denning, 2011b, p. 148)

Although that story has little to do with church life, it makes a clear connection between using money and a person's values, and highlights how it's not possible to merely bale out of a relationship. The same is true for churches. The shared values in congregational life are embodied and communicated through the approach to money and finance. For example: How are stewardship campaigns run? What kind of response is given to questions about church finances? To whom does a church give money? How is that organized? These are just some of the questions that convey the values of a particular church and they will inevitably become a crucial part of the ongoing narrative ecology of a church.

As we have seen, the financial challenges that a building makes upon a church's ministry and its organizational narrative can be extensive, so we turn to explore how a building's architecture can also shape its improvised storytelling.

Architecture

The narrative power of church architecture is clearly apparent in the number of weddings that any particular building hosts. If a church has a steady stream of smiling brides, grooms and their supporting entourages then it has the architectural draw with which people wish to be associated. They wish to write that church building into their story as a couple and as individuals. Churches that are less architecturally attractive may still have some weddings but the reasons will be different – for instance, it is the local church linked to the community school or the one that the bride/groom attended as a child or presently worships at. The story may then be about the building as the place where 'I was christened' or 'We had Nan's funeral'.

Cathedral architecture can work in those ways as well but there are additional story lines within the narrative processes; for example, it is a physical reality that speaks through its very presence. Thus, the gothic architecture of the National Cathedral in Washington DC is making a direct connection between the story of its contemporary ministry and the story of British and European Christianity from which the Episcopal Church has evolved. Architecture also functions at the level of organizational metaphor. It is often used as an image for organizations and their designs, which works around ideas of plans and structures. However, as Weick observes:

While the metaphor of architecture is a compelling model for organizational change, it is not the only one . . . an alternative metaphor, design as improvisational theatre, corrects many of the blind spots induced by the metaphor of architecture. (Weick, 2001, pp. 57–8)

The architecture of churches and cathedrals sets aspects of their organizational storytelling in stone, which is a very powerful form of narrative and makes improvisation harder. Nevertheless, like all stories it can be reframed and retold. We have already discussed examples of this in the reordering at Leicester and the removal of scaffolding at Salisbury, both of which weave together the buildings' architecture and their stories. John Witcombe, the Dean of Coventry, spoke in conversation about how unyielding the cathedral felt and of his desire to introduce some 'flex' into it. He did not feel he had succeeded thus far, but was mindful of the advice not to do battle with the building as it would always win.

The architectural stories of local churches can be equally powerful in their communal settings. We noted this in Chapter 7 while looking at historical stories and how the demolition of the original Victorian church of All Saints and its replacement with a modern structure continued to have a strong impact upon the story told about the church in the neighbourhood. It is not just the external architecture that is important. Over the turn of the millennium Vaughan was vicar for a team of rural churches. One of those churches had replaced its organ around ten years before, which involved a prominent set of organ pipes extending into a side chapel. One day in the visitors' book there was an anguished complaint about this musical intrusion into the chapel from someone who had returned to visit the church. Part of the pain was because the chapel was where this person had undergone her service of 'churching' following the birth of her children. This is a service from the old prayer book that has fallen out of use: in his 30 years of ministry Vaughan has never had a request for it. Nevertheless, that individual's story gives a sense of how church architecture and a sense of place can have such a strong effect on people that it is no surprise that any reordering of church buildings can be hugely controversial and have a long-lasting narrative impact.

Governance

Wherever lay people or clergy from a particular denomination gather for a period of time, it will not be long before conversation turns towards stories about governance. We have Methodist friends who will happily share experiences that illustrate the organizational pros and cons of 'Conference'; Baptist friends who will share their stories of 'preaching with a view' and the power of a local church; and Presbyterian friends who describe the 'presbytery as our bishop' and what that means for their system of governance.

Our experience is mostly formed by the Church of England; and to get an understanding of the demands the Church of England makes in this area of its narrative ecology a good place to start is James Behrens' volume *Practical Church Management*, in particular Chapter 1, 'Who's Who'. This sets out in detail the definitions of, and the *dramatis personae* involved in, a regular parish church. For instance, under the first sub-heading of The Diocese, there is: the diocesan parsonages board, diocesan advisory committee, diocesan board of finance, bishop, suffragan bishop, archdeacon, provincial episcopal visitor, diocesan secretary, diocesan registrar, diocesan surveyor, diocesan synod. And there are further, comprehensive sub-headings for The Deanery, The Parish and Rules in a Christian Community (Behrens, 1998, pp. 3–16). Governance for the smallest church in England is complex, and even more so for the larger bodies such as cathedrals.

Nicolas Alldrit has identified four historic models of cathedral community: (1) Semi-Monastic Canons – bishop and clergy leading a common life; (2) St Augustine's Rule – bishop and clergy living a common monastic life; (3) St Benedict's Monasticism – the Rule of St Benedict applied to the common life of bishop and clergy; (4) The Prebendal System – cathedrals with clergy in roles as deans, precentors, chancellors and treasurers who were supported financially by prebendal gifts (Alldrit, 1998, pp. 35–49). Alldrit argues that in England only the prebendal model survived the Reformation although in much modified form. In addition to these historic models, the Church of England has added what might be called the Parish Church model where large parish churches have been made cathedrals, most usually for new dioceses.

A cathedral's organizational narrative about governance will be improvised around its origins – monastic, prebendal or parish – and, although there are no longer any monastic cathedrals in the Church of England, there can still be important elements of that history in their improvised stories, such as a daily round of services and a commitment to aspects of St Benedict's Rule (de Waal, 1990). This takes us back to the historical narratives identified in Chapter 7 and how these continue to have a significant impact upon the ongoing improvised stories. Of course, more recently founded denominations can have an equally diverse narrative ecology of governance. The various stories told by worldwide Methodism are a good example.

We have already explored the narrative complexity of governance in the Church of England with reference to a collegiate church in Chapter 6 and a proprietary chapel in the introduction to Chapter 7. Churches of one particular strand can be drawn into the intricacy of another's story, and Local Ecumenical Projects are a good example of this. At a very local level in Warwick one Anglican church, St Nicholas, was looking to sell off its parish hall. It was situated behind the neighbouring Baptist church, which was interested in purchasing it. The hall had originally been given to St Nicholas for educational purposes and could only be used to that end. The same charitable protocols had to remain in place when ownership was transferred from Anglicans to Baptists.

Pastoral

Improvised narratives under this heading come in many forms and perhaps the most common are those that deal with pastoral care and organizational conflict. In themselves these can be difficult and sensitive matters which raise awkward questions. How can people be encouraged to be caring without, at the same time, engendering guilt or resentment? Is it possible to enable a church or congregation to reflect on possible areas of conflict without generating more discord and disagreement? Sometimes it can be appropriate to use stories that are drawn from the life experiences of those within the group, but there are also risks in using biographical (or autobiographical) details: they can be delicate or tricky in pastoral concerns or appear to take sides in disagreements when the role of the leader might be best served by helping a church to reflect upon how to live and work with difference and conflict. What follows are two stories that Vaughan has used at various times in his ministry to encourage congregations in that journey of discovery and resolution.

The first, from Donald Capps' work on reframing in pastoral care, recounts a story from Paul Watzlawick and Richard Fisch's work on problem resolution. It tells of how, 'during one of many nineteenth century riots in Paris, the commander of an army detachment received orders to clear a city square by firing at the rabble'.

> He commanded his soldiers to take up firing positions, their rifles levelled at the crowd. As a ghastly silence descended, he drew his sword and shouted at the top of his voice: 'Ladies and gentlemen, I have orders to fire at the rabble. But as I see a great number of honest, respectable citizens before me, I request that they leave so that I can safely shoot the rabble.' The square was empty in a few minutes. (Capps, 1990, p. 17)

Capps goes on to explore various narratives in which the process of reframing can resolve pastoral conflict.

The second story comes from the Lutheran pastor William R. White and his tale of two brothers, which he describes as a Jewish folk story:

> There were once two brothers who farmed together. They shared equally in all of the work and split the profits exactly. Each had his own granary. One of the brothers was married and had a large family; the other brother was single. One day the single brother thought to himself, 'It's not fair that we divide the grain evenly. My brother has many mouths to feed, while I have but one. I know what I'll do, I will take a sack of grain from my

granary each evening and put it in my brother's granary.' So, each night when it was dark, he carefully carried a sack of grain, placing it in his brother's barn.

Now the married brother thought to himself, 'It's not fair that we divide the grain evenly. I have many children to care for me in my old age, and my brother has none. I know what I'll do, I will take a sack of grain from my granary each evening and put it in my brother's granary.' So he did. And each morning the two brothers were amazed to discover that though they had removed a sack of grain the night before, they still had just as many.

One night the two brothers met each other halfway between their barns, each carrying a sack of grain. Then they understood the mystery. And they embraced, and loved each other deeply. It's said that God looked down from heaven, saw the two brothers embracing, and said, 'I declare this to be a holy place, for I have witnessed extraordinary love here.' It's also said it was on that spot that Solomon built the first temple. (White, 1986, pp. 30–1)

Those involved in church life can immediately think of ways in which they might apply these and other pastorally orientated stories. They can help groups of people reflect on their shared life together. Of course, they can also be used on a more individual level. The pastoral use of narrative is not just about conflict. We have already referred to this in thinking about the relationship between architecture and story. When a wedding couple writes a church building into their personal narrative it is also functioning as a pastoral story. When bereaved families come to a church for a funeral or service of thanksgiving, very often they want to tell stories about the person they knew and loved. And if they come back to church for a significant anniversary it is the ongoing pastoral story that is drawing them back.

In a three-part programme produced by the BBC on Canterbury Cathedral in 2014 and subsequently released on DVD, the Cathedral's Canon Pastor talks about how the cathedral has more meaning for her now that it is filled with stories and memories of people whom she has welcomed and met there.[4] Such improvised storytelling and biographical layering is essential to organizational life, and the role of those leading is to ensure that the ongoing sharing of tales is as healthy as possible.

Mission

The comprehensive historical and theological survey of Christian mission undertaken by the South African missiologist David J. Bosch uses Hans Küng's six periods of Christian history, or 'paradigms', to set out the Church's different approaches to mission over time. In Bosch's thinking these are: (1) The apocalyptic paradigm of primitive Christianity; (2) The Hellenistic paradigm of the patristic period; (3) the medieval Roman Catholic paradigm; (4) the Protestant (Reformation) paradigm; (5) the modern Enlightenment paradigm; (6) the emerging ecumenical paradigm (Bosch, 1991, pp. 181–2; see also Küng, 1995). He notes that in each of these periods a wide variety of Christians wrestled with their understanding of the faith. In his view, 'all of them believed and argued that their understanding of the faith and the church's mission was faithful to God's intent. This did not, however, mean that they all thought alike and came to the same conclusions' (Bosch, 1991, p. 182). Within our narrative approach to church ministry, these can be seen as different iterations of the ecclesial story discussed in Chapter 6, and they already highlight the diversity of understanding in the Church regarding mission.

Given that the ecclesial story of mission is diverse, it is perhaps no surprise that there is a wide variety of views when it comes to improvised stories. We get a sense of this by looking briefly at the work of Ann Morisy on mission. She argues: 'Story is like currency in that it can change hands without losing value. The telling of a story hands it over to others, who in turn can tell it to other people. This ability is quite extraordinary' (Morisy, 2004, p. 69). Within the context of mission, she believes that certain stories have a particular potency; one example she returns to is that of a Mothers' Union branch shipping sewing machines to women in Zimbabwe (p. 62). She calls these 'generative stories', which are 'the often unacknowledged but potent events that help to make people different' (p. 73).

For Morisy the value of developing story-rich lives in churches is three-fold. First, it enables people to understand the gospel more fully; second, it encourages links beyond the usual networks of family and friends; and third, it enables those who are older to share their wisdom with younger generations. In summary, she believes:

> This capacity for story to shape people's lives in the direction of the Kingdom of God and of Jesus needs to be taken seriously because it addresses so many of our hopes and fears in relation to mission in a post-modern context. (Morisy, p. 90)

This relates directly to the insights from Bosch. Whether or not we wish to describe the contemporary world as 'post-modern', it is clear that history and culture change over time and one of the profound challenges of mission is to understand those changes and address them. Within that context mission happens in different arenas and can therefore take on different forms, but one of the shared characteristics of those various manifestations of outreach will be that they are stories being told, stories being shared and stories being understood.[5]

Education

When we examined the nature of the Church in Chapter 6, we touched on Wenger's idea of community of practice (Wenger, 1998) and noted that this has been applied to churches, in particular by Clive Marsh and John Fitzmaurice. Both Marsh and Fitzmaurice also apply Wenger's concept of reification to the life of the Church. Human beings belong to different social groups and reification is the process whereby we 'record and display evidence of our participation in such communities in all sorts of ways' (Marsh, 2006, p. 145).

Fitzmaurice traces this journey of reification through the sacramental life of the Church:

> The Word becomes flesh/material, the experience is narrated into a story which is written down in a book, the story is condensed into a meal; renewal is marked with symbolic washing, drowning

and rebirth; the invisible actions of the Holy Spirit are made visible with the anointing of oil. (Fitzmaurice, 2016, p. 103)

Marsh and Fitzmaurice see this as a shared process of negotiating identity and meaning, which links directly to Ladkins' insights into meaning-making as a jointly negotiated activity with which we began this chapter.

It is our contention that storytelling and story sharing are foundational to being a community of practice and that how people participate in communal narratives is crucial to leadership and followership in churches. Thus, as Carroll argues, leadership in the Body of Christ is also a *joint* enterprise (Carroll, 2011, p. 84) or what Fancourt calls 'church-in-dialogue' (Fancourt 2013, p. 123).

In his insightful volume on leadership and wisdom, Michael Sadgrove outlines how the quest for meaning, or what he calls the 'art of interpretation', is at the heart of wisdom. This form of wisdom requires an openness to how we are being prepared to discover 'patterns, connections and meanings' (Sadgrove, 2008, p. 40). The Church has always been involved in the world of education, whether formally through schools, colleges and universities, or with its own programmes of learning. Openness to shared sensemaking and conversations about meaning are inextricably part of communities of practice in education and the Church.

One story that is used by Donna Brandes and Paul Ginnis in their work on student-centred learning can help churches in developing a willingness to be open and self-reflective.

Once an old man sat by the side of a road, in the shade of a tree and gazing off into the distance, contemplating . . . who knows-what? Along came a stranger who stopped to pass the time of day, putting down his bundle and taking out a ham sandwich and a bottle of wine, which he forgot to share with the old man. During conversation, the stranger pointed to the village nestled in the valley below, and asked, 'What are the people like down there? I'm just moving to that village.'

The old man lay back in the shade of the tree, and threw the question back, 'What were they like in the place where you used to live, my friend?'

A thundercloud seemed to pass over the stranger's face: 'Oh they were rogues of the worst sort – a pack of knaves! Never could get a kind word out of any of them.'

The old man shook his head in the shade of the tree and spoke, 'Well then, that's what the people are like in that village down there, my son.' The stranger heaved himself to his feet and walked sadly down the hill. The old man leaned back against the tree for his siesta.

Later, when he woke, he saw another stranger approaching. The newcomer smiled, and asked if he could share the shade of the tree so the old man made room for him, and gratefully accepted the stranger's offer of some cheese. As they chatted, the stranger pointed to the village below: 'What are the people like down there?' he asked, 'I'm thinking of moving to that village soon.'

A twinkle, unobserved, appeared in the old man's eye, as once again he parried the question: 'What were they like where you've just come from, my friend?' The stranger's face lit up. 'Oh, they're wonderful people, salt of the earth, not a harsh word nor a dishonest act have I heard of these many years. I only wish I could stay, but it's time for me to move on.' The old man hid his delight by lying back in the shade, as he responded, 'Well, I'm glad to say that's exactly how you'll find those people in the village below.' (Brandes and Ginnis, 1986, pp. 214–15)

This story connects with John Inge's analysis of cathedrals and education (Platten and Lewis, 2006, pp. 26–38) where he uses the metaphor of a journey to describe how cathedrals can be part of people's educational and other pilgrimage by providing a sense of wonder and mystery. He says this can be achieved through regular worship, sharing the Christian story and improvised events. In essence, cathedrals as sacred spaces should be available as a resource that is 'educational in the broadest sense in that they enable people to reflect upon their experience in a godly setting, which is what I have argued the education offered by cathedrals should be about' (Inge in Platten and Lewis, p. 36). We would argue that this idea can be applied much more widely across the whole life of the Church.

Media

As we remarked in Chapter 6, Christianity has been a storytelling religion since its beginning and emerged from the storytelling faith of Judaism. We have explored the importance of 'big picture', interpretive narratives but how do they work at the level of improvised stories? Conant and Norgaard have used the term 'touchpoints' for those small, everyday interactions that are important for leaders and followers in organizations (Conant and Norgaard 2011). These can be planned or spontaneous, casual or carefully choreographed. As part of the process of leaders embodying their personal and organizational values, they urge their readers 'to forget about Powerpoint slides and tell more stories' because compelling stories are what bring those values to life (Conant and Norgaard, p. 116).

Steven Croft has made a similar observation about leadership in churches. He comments that it is 'not only about a great set of speeches or major decisions about vision or direction'.

> Leadership is exercised through face to face meetings and phone conversations, through thousands of emails, through blogs and articles, through the way we answer questions and respond to dissent. Leadership is about influencing others and one of the key ways leaders exercise influence is through our words and the way we use them. (Croft, 2016, p. 47)

A wide variety of media is now available for sharing words and telling stories.

Churches have always communicated their stories through different forms of media – including traditional media such as stained glass, drama, music and books, and newer forms such as radio, TV and social media. A good example is the three-part programme produced by the BBC on Canterbury Cathedral, already mentioned. The programmes told stories relating to the cathedral communities, such as the clergy team, choirs, stonemasons, gardeners and volunteers, together with those who came to be part of the cathedral's life at certain times, such as the Archbishop of Canterbury, clergy from across the Anglican Communion, and visitors. The introductions to the three episodes differ but each contains the bold narrative claim that 'the *story* of Canterbury Cathedral is the *story* of England'. Another literary reference occurs in the final episode when Jocelyn Prebble, retiring from the Events Office, describes entering the cathedral precincts as like entering the imagination of C. S. Lewis: 'You come through from Canterbury and it's like Narnia' (episode 3, 46 minutes 36–41 seconds).

The place that this form of improvised narrative has in the life of Canterbury is illustrated throughout the series, so two examples must suffice. In episode 2, the Precentor is interviewed about his role and makes clear the storied nature of ministry at the cathedral:

> [T]he great thing about this place is that you've 1400 years of this story and it's continuing. It's not showing any signs of people not coming to this church, as we'll see over Easter hopefully. And, to be a part of that narrative – a tiny, insignificant part – but a part of that narrative is incredible. (episode 2, 12 minutes 17–41 seconds)

Something similar is true in local churches as well. The presence in churches of boards with names of previous clergy, of stone tablets with past worshippers, or new items of furniture bearing a donor's name on a plaque are all examples of people being written into the narrative of a church. This static and traditional form of story presently runs alongside many other forms: newsletters and magazines; websites and social media; local newspapers, radio and television; and for some (such as Canterbury Cathedral) national and international coverage as well.

Art

We have already touched upon one form of artistic story in churches when we considered architecture as an improvised narrative. Naturally, there are many other expressions too – music and artworks are perhaps the most obvious. In his work on the origins of religion, Robert N. Bellah contends that religion, narrative, music and art have been inextricably linked since the dawn of human evolution, and uses Lévi-Strauss's concept of 'total story' to bring these cultural expressions together (Bellah, 2011, p. 33). In his exploration of music and theology Don E. Saliers sees music as a form of 'living practice' (Saliers, 2007, pp. 12–15) which is akin to religion.

Although Saliers does not make a connection with Wenger's communities of practice, they would seem to be in the same vicinity. And in her analysis of music *as* theology, Maeve Louise Heaney argues that music mediates faith in three ways, through: (1) present moments of transcendence; (2) shared presence with God and friends; and (3) a physical embodiment of Christ's presence. Neither Saliers nor Heaney explicitly discusses the relationship between music and story but they do see music as both a communal and a theological activity.

We would agree with this analysis and therefore argue that there will inevitably be a great deal of storytelling and story sharing with music in churches. The music created for worship will link directly to the interpretive stories (theological, ecclesial, liturgical) outlined in Chapter 6. There will be a history of the choir and its directors of music and, if a choir has been disbanded by a vicar and church council in favour of a music group, then there is likely to be a contested identity story (history, personal, organizational) about the role of music in that church. The ongoing place of music in congregational life will be an improvised story that may well link to other ongoing narratives, such as finance (can we afford the musical provision?), architecture (will there be reordering of the building?), mission and media (is our music communicating our understanding of the gospel as effectively as we wish?) and others.

If we turn to physical artwork in the form of painting and sculpture, we can see how the context for the improvised story is shaped by the interpretive stories that we explored in Chapter 6. We can take as one example the crucifixion of Christ, which is one of the most powerful images in Christianity and western culture. It can be surprising to learn that it took centuries to be formalized in visual terms. Marcia Kupfer notes that the Emperor Constantine used plentiful state resources to recapitulate selected episodes of the Passion story: Christ in the Garden of Gethsemane, the kiss of Judas, Christ's arrest, Peter's denial, Christ before Annas and Caiaphas, Christ before Pilate, Pilate washing his hands, Simon of Cyrene bearing the cross, the crowning with thorns. At the same time, however, the earliest Christian art eschewed any depiction of Christ crucified. (Kupfer, 2008, p. 5)

Thus, we can see that story is at the heart of Christian art, but what stories are depicted and why are more complex questions.

Brock and Parker have made a similar observation about the long gestation of images of the crucifixion within Christian art and explored some implications for a theology of paradise within the organizational politics of the Church (Brock and Parker, 2008, p. ix). Naturally, the process of what David Morgan calls 'the sacred gaze' is a multifaceted process, which can involve four elements: seeing what is there, seeing what one expects to be there, seeing what one desires to be there and seeing what one is told is there (Morgan, 2005, p. 74). This in turn engages with all the interpretive and identity stories that we have discussed in the previous two chapters. Therefore, as we might imagine, the scope for improvised storytelling around church artwork is considerable.

Keith Walker begins his analysis of images in cathedrals with a story about the cross and one person's response to a crucifix in church (Walker, 1998). He recounts how a woman in some distress from a recent bereavement wandered into Winchester Cathedral and found solace in a wooden sculpture of Christ's crucifixion by the artist Peter Eugene Ball. Walker notes that such experiences 'remind us of why cathedrals are built and suggest the power of their form and contents' (p. 105). He goes on to place the musical and visual arts that are most often employed in cathedrals within the three interpretive stories outlined earlier. The context for all art within cathedrals is that of a liturgical space 'which reaches its consummation in the celebration of the Eucharist' (p. 106).

To put it another way, cathedrals and churches provide sacred spaces for acting out the theological story of Christian identity, and the various artistic expressions found within those buildings illustrate and highlight those stories. In addition, Walker briefly relates the ecclesial story of church art through medieval culture, Reformation conflicts, the artistic fluctuations of Enlightenment, Romanticism and Tractarianism, to the close of the twentieth century with its emphasis on conserving the artistic story rather than encouraging new expressions of it. Once again the improvised stories around a church's or cathedral's artistic culture will certainly relate to the other improvised narratives around finance, governance, education, media and quite possibly more.

Untended stories

Finally, there is a further category of improvised storytelling in all organizations which is also present in churches – those untended stories within a narrative ecology such as gossip, jokes and untold stories. They have not been given their own bounded circle in Figure 4 because they tend to exist in an organization's narrative 'gaps'. Such things may seem relatively insignificant when set against the improvised story of finance, or the identity story of a church's history, or the interpretive story of Christ's life and ministry, but, as Conant and Norgaard make clear in their analysis of organizational interactions, even the smallest encounter 'is spring-loaded with possibilities. Each one can build – or break – a relationship. Even a brief interaction can change the way people think about themselves, their leaders, and their future' (Conant and Norgaard, 2011, p. 9).

The same is true about an untold story or an apparently throw-away metaphor. For instance, in one conversation a dean described another dean as the 'Velveteen Rabbit'. It may have been a term of affection drawing upon the image of Margery Williams' children's story. But the level of organizational meaning in that storied reference can be enormous, as we explored when looking at organizational narratives in Chapter 7 (Sims, 2004) – so even a storied image used consciously in one way can have hidden depths of organizational meaning.

Summary and conclusion

We began this chapter with Donna Ladkin's insight that organizational meaning-making is negotiated and iterative, and we have argued throughout that much of this process takes place through story and narrative. We believe that for churches the day-to-day storytelling and story sharing which we call improvised stories takes place around eight key areas: (1) Finance; (2) Architecture; (3) Governance; (4) Pastoral; (5) Mission; (6) Education; (7) Media and (8) Art. These eight narrative spheres have been set out diagrammatically in Figure 4 (see page 128) and then explored in more detail, including the additional narrative form of 'Untended stories' which roams free across all the spheres.

In mapping out practical expressions of these improvised stories we have drawn primarily on our own experience and we hope that readers will have been calling to mind their own examples of improvisation. For us some of the key questions that emerge at this point for potential leaders as we reflect upon improvised stories include:

1　Who are the key partners with whom you are negotiating the story of the church that you serve?
2　Which of these storytelling areas do you feel confident in and which less so? What happens to the stories in those spheres where we are less confident?
3　Are there other forms of improvised narrative from your own experience that can be identified?

Chapters 6, 7 and 8 have explored what types of story are told within churches as they engage in the process of organizational sensemaking and how those different forms of narrative interact. We have argued that we can see: (1) Interpretive stories of theology, ecclesiology and liturgy framing the broader narrative stage; (2) Identity stories of history, organization and personal narrative providing the storied core in any specific context; and both of these shape (3) the Improvised stories of lived experience which emerge from this larger narrative flux.

We would place this approach within an understanding of human beings as narrative creatures (Bellah, 2011), Christianity as a storytelling faith (MacCulloch, 2009) and churches as storytelling communities of practice (Smith, 2009, 2013). The way that we tell stories is one of the ways in which we create and manage meaning as individuals and communities. Several writers on leadership (Ladkin; Alvesson and Spicer; Hurst; Mead) have observed how a primary task of leadership is to enable organizational meaning, and that will involve supporting, enabling and influencing the telling of an organization's story.

In the light of this, it is important to understand how churches work and undertake their processes of narrative sensemaking, so we have explored how that plays out in the types of story that churches tell about their ministry. In her discussion of management and play Margaret Wheatley affirms the idea of storytellers. She says that we are great weavers of tales, listening intently around the campfire to see which stories best capture our imagination and the experience of our lives (Wheatley, 2006, p. 214). One of the deans we spoke with said that part of the dean's role is to spot opportunities and take them. While we agree with that statement, the insight does not only apply in cathedral ministry. We would argue that telling the story of each opportunity and linking it to a church's organizational narrative is crucial for all churches.

As David Hurst has observed in his work on leadership (drawing on the narrative of the exodus from Egypt by the Children of Israel):

[S]tory and metaphor are the medium of leadership – it is the way in which homo sapiens has made sense of complexity for thousands of years, and today it is the way in which leaders make meaning for people and define their organization's reality. (Hurst, 2012, p. 97)

However, one of the dangers of seeing this as solely the task of leaders is that it potentially falls into what Kellerman calls the 'leadercentric' nature of much thinking in this field (Kellerman, 2008). She presses for a better understanding of the different types of follower (bystanders, participants, activists, diehards).

Leaders and followers are not mutually exclusive binaries but often part of a much more nuanced organizational narrative. Kellerman quotes the story of William Wilberforce and the end of the slave trade as an example of leaders and followers collaborating (Kellerman, 2008, p. 259). In the next section we examine a case study of how storytelling and sharing can still have a significant effect upon church life even when that is being driven by quantitative and managerialist assumptions, as we explore how the Natural Church Development (NCD) programme has been applied in one local church. In particular we shall look at how that relates to the metaphor of narrative ecology from Chapter 4; the image of curating stories from Chapter 5 and the notions of interpretive, identity and improvised stories from Chapters 6, 7 and 8.

Questions

1 Which is (or are) the most significant improvised stories in your particular situation?
2 Is there a particular field of improvised narrative that you have noticed to be complex across different local churches that you have been involved with? Are there similar reasons for that?
3 Can you think of other areas of improvised storytelling from your church experience?

Notes

1 http://torch.ox.ac.uk/narrative-and-proof-two-sides-same-equation-0 where du Sautoy is the keynote speaker for a panel of respondents, organized by The Oxford Research Centre in the Humanities. Du Sautoy's lecture starts at 7 minutes 10 seconds, accessed 30.3.2017.
2 Du Sautoy develops his understanding of mathematical narrative through a metaphor of journey, including the journey of Frodo from the Shire to Mordor (J. R. R. Tolkien), and the game of chess, while drawing upon Roland Barthes's *S/Z: An essay* (1970) and alluding to Christopher Booker's *The Seven Basic Plots* (2004).

3 The Salisbury Cathedral Strategy for 2013–17 and Programme for 2015/16 is available online here: www.salisburycathedral.org.uk/sites/default/files/Salisbury%20Cathedral%20Strategy%20and%20Programme_2015_16.pdf, accessed 30.3.2017.

4 *Canterbury Cathedral: A BBC documentary that gives a unique look behind the scenes of Canterbury Cathedral* (London: BBC, 2014). Episode 3, 4 minutes 10–24 seconds. In Vaughan's conversation with the Dean, Robert Willis, he observed how there were some stories included about which even he was unaware.

5 Further reflection on how story works in contrasting approaches to mission (through a traditional evangelistic event and a Christmas Tree festival) can be found in Roberts 2017.

9

Curating Congregational Stories in a Tick Box Church?

Introduction

This chapter provides a case study on the ideas and thinking that we have set out in our book. In terms of Barthes's distinction between 'readerly' and 'writerly' texts it is a writerly narrative in the sense that numerous voices have been involved in creating this account, producing what Boje calls a multi-authored story. But what is it a story about? At one level, this is a narrative about 'managerialism' in the sense described by Martin Parker in his book *Against Management* (2002). He argues that management has become the new civic religion and its three main strands are control over nature, control over humans and control over organizational abilities or technologies.

These forms of control ensure that things happen, give us a particular kind of progress and defeat disorder. Of course, such an approach brings a number of benefits. For instance, they consist of processes that are reasonably certain, less arbitrary than earlier ways of organizing, and therefore fairer. It is also possible to check whether these processes have been followed, so you can control the controllers with less risk of incompetence, dishonesty and abuse on the part of others. They give you formulae by which you can tell what you should be paying attention to next.

Having said that there are also hazards and downsides. In a growing body of literature the most well-known critique comes from George Ritzer's work on 'McDonaldization' (1993) which was applied to churches by John Drane in his book *The McDonaldization of the Church* (2000). And this critical approach can be found more recently in volumes like *The Dark Side of Transformational Leadership* (2013) by Dennis Tourish and *The Stupidity Paradox* (2016) by Mats Alvesson and André Spicer. The language of strategy, planning and effectiveness can be used to exercise unaccountable control and power, as well as hiding missteps and mistakes.

We shall explore some of these dynamics in this chapter as we provide an account of the way in which a managerialist approach to ministry called Natural Church Development (NCD) was introduced into a Church of England diocese and, more specifically, how that relates to a narrative approach to congregational life. Although this story takes place within a particular denomination, we believe the issues and lessons have a wider application in other churches and countries and, indeed, in other organizations. We begin by outlining the NCD programme before looking at how one church implemented it. Then we shall examine how this maps on to the notions of narrative ecology, different forms of church storytelling and the idea of curating stories in churches.

What is NCD?

Since 2010 the Diocese of Coventry has been using the ideas outlined by the NCD programme as its principal means of approaching local ministry and achieving church growth. This system is based on the research of Christian Schwarz into what characteristics are shared by healthy churches. The eight qualities identified in his work are: (1) Empowering leadership; (2) Gift-orientated ministry; (3) Passionate spirituality; (4) Effective structures; (5) Inspiring worship; (6) Holistic small groups; (7) Need-orientated outreach; and (8) Loving relationships.

The diocesan website introduces the process in this way:

> The Diocesan core strategy is to help every church grow and develop in the eight essential quality characteristics (8EQs) of healthy growing churches. This approach is based on the most extensive research of church health ever undertaken across the

world by the Natural Church Development Institute led by Christian Schwarz, a German theologian.[1]

Arguably the language used to describe this programme contains a significant organizational tension. On the one hand, it describes the process in terms of nature and growth. For instance:

It is a different way of thinking and at its heart is the Scriptural picture of the church as a living organism in which God gives the growth. It encourages us to think about the church (the body of Christ) as a living organism and about how we can work with God to facilitate the healthy qualitative growth of the church.

Yet on the other hand, the means of analysing this growth is thoroughly quantitative or managerialist. It sees causes and consequences as a mechanism rather than as an organism, and seems only to be interested in the measurable. Thus: 'One of the main tools NCD provides is a survey which is taken by a representative sample of a church's membership each year or so. This provides accurate and detailed information on which to base sound decisions for future action.'[2]

A significant sentence on the website about NCD is the claim about the breadth of this approach: 'Its universal principles are applicable regardless of culture, denomination or churchmanship.'[3] The claim for universality is a bold one and implicitly rests on two forms of authority – biblical language and objective measurement. We shall come back to the tension between metaphors of organic growth and numerical assessment later in this chapter after examining the process of the programme in more detail.

Another key element in NCD is the six stages of the 8EQs cycle, which are: (1) Testing; (2) Understanding; (3) Planning; (4) Doing; (5) Experiencing; (6) Perceiving. In the next section we give an account of how one church went about implementing this cycle. This was the church where Vaughan is the minister and although it is his version of the story, it remains necessary to bring critical analysis and questions to his qualitative narrative of events which also includes many voices from the local congregation.

The story of St Mary's first NCD cycle[4]

Taking the survey

The NCD programme requires each church to identify a group to oversee the process. This can be a new body that is formed specifically for this task or an existing committee that is given oversight. It was decided that the first NCD cycle would be overseen by the church council's standing committee, consisting of the incumbent (Vaughan), churchwardens, church administrator, treasurer and church council secretary. An NCD mentor was also appointed to work with the committee at all stages of the cycle. To begin with it was agreed that Vaughan would introduce the initiative by preaching an introductory sermon to explain the process and the first survey, which would then be completed afterwards at The Rectory with refreshments. In doing so we explored how the language and metaphors that we use to talk about church life shape our understanding of the nature of the Church and its leadership. It was noted in the sermon how Scripture uses different images for the Church (for instance, 'vine' in John 15; 'body' in 1 Corinthians 12; 'foundations' in Matthew 7), and how in secular organizations using the language of, for example, gardening and growth is likely to produce a very different shared culture from that of, say, superhero or robot.[5]

Vaughan believes that it is important for clergy to be open and transparent about their thoughts and feelings in the process of leading church stories. So in the conclusion to his introductory sermon he stated:

Paradoxically, the NCD programme isn't necessarily about change, rather it's about asking whether we can do things better. Speaking personally, I admit to having reservations. For instance, I've doubts about the claim that these principles work for all churches, everywhere, at all times. In my experience, one size doesn't usually fit all. So, why then, should *we* engage?

First, there's a healthy degree of honesty in that the programme doesn't claim to be a silver bullet which will solve all our problems. That's good and realistic. Second, it is a tool for us to use in assessing where we are and what we might need to improve. That's also very helpful, especially as we need to look seriously at having a stewardship campaign in the next 18 months. We have these about every five years and if we're asking people to fund the ministry of St Mary's, then all of us need to have confidence that what we're funding is in good health and what we need. And third (which brings us back to the beginning of my sermon and again speaking personally) I like the NCD language which speaks about *quality* rather than *quantity*.

After the service, a cross-section of the church was invited to fill in the survey forms. The forms start with a series of questions (Q1–Q6) which ask for respondents' personal details (such as age group, gender, and how long they have been part of this church). Then they present a series of 85 statements (Q7–Q91) and ask those being surveyed to rate their level of agreement with each one as: 'very great extent', 'great extent', 'average', 'hardly', or 'not at all'. Thus, for example, the first statement (Q7) reads: 'I feel my task in our church is a positive challenge that stretches my faith'; and the final one (Q91) is: 'The activities of our church are well planned and organised.' As a result, each of the eight qualities is measured by 10 or 11 of these metrics and the weakest becomes the focus for improvement in the coming year.

We also gave out cards to everyone in church so that anyone could share their thoughts on the scheme and people were invited to email their thoughts to the vicar as well. The survey results came through just before Christmas and the headline scores are set out in Figure 5. In the New Year the standing committee began to consider its response and how to take the process forward, bearing in mind that the cycle was clear in its expectation that the weakest category would be the one that needed addressing. The metaphor used for this by the NCD literature is a barrel, and the argument it makes is that the maximum quantity such a container could hold is fixed by its shortest stave.

Processing the results

As with many in the Church of England, the weakest category in this church was Passionate Spirituality. The standing committee felt

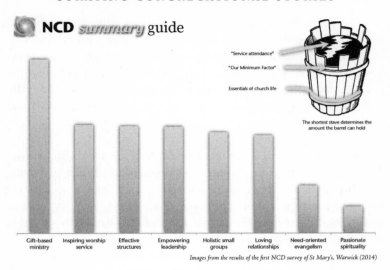

NCD *summary* guide

Images from the results of the first NCD survey of St Mary's, Warwick (2014)

Figure 5: Quality Characteristic Summary Guide (December 2014).

strongly that a collaborative approach to these results would be better than a top–down response. This would involve feeding back the results to everyone and inviting any who wished to be involved in the next stage to participate in it. The plan was for Vaughan as the incumbent to preach a series of four sermons for the various congregations at St Mary's during Lent outlining the challenges involved with Passionate Spirituality. This would be followed up after Easter with discussion groups and lunch in church after the main morning service. Once again, there would be cards for everyone to input their thoughts and comments into the NCD process if they wished.

With the first Lent sermon the church gave out copies of the three-page summary guide of the survey results (including the graphic in Figure 5). Vaughan preached on the overall outcomes and explained the next stage of the 8EQ cycle and how it would be approached at St Mary's. This included celebrating our strongest categories and identifying our weakest.

In conclusion, Vaughan asked:

Where does this survey of the eight essential qualities for a healthy church leave us at St Mary's? There are two key outcomes: first, we *are* a healthy church and there's much to give thanks to God for; and second, we do have some areas of ministry which need developing and we'll be looking at those in the weeks to come.

Finally let me suggest three questions we might like to reflect upon at this stage. These could frame our responses for our cards but, equally, you may wish to address something else that's occurred in your mind and that's perfectly fine. Three closing questions then:

1 What do we make of the process: of looking at St Mary's ministry in this way; of seeking improvements and then reviewing what we've achieved?
2 What do we make of the survey results: from your experience are they a fair reflection of the life and ministry of this church, or has something been missed out or obscured?
3 What do we make of the barrel analogy, which is fundamental to the 8EQ process: is that a helpful way to proceed?

The remaining sermons looked at three of the weaker responses to survey questions under the Passionate Spirituality heading. These were: Q29 – I know that other church members pray for me regularly; Q68 – I firmly believe that God will work even more powerfully in our church in the coming years; Q84 – I enjoy reading the Bible on my own. Thus, the three remaining sermons explored are Prayer, Bible Reading and Lived Experience of God. Cards continued to be available for everyone to have an opportunity to have their say and they could either be given in as part of the offertory collection or returned to the church office later in the week.

The next stage on the journey

On the Sunday following the final sermon we arranged for a light lunch in church and, for those who wished to stay, a chance to work on how to address those three weaker areas of Prayer, Bible Reading and Lived Experience of God identified from the survey by the standing committee. To do this we used work sheets adapted from *Change Teams* (a programme for school development).[6] There was a sheet for each of the topics which sought to identify up to three actions for each heading and who would take those forward. One person was asked beforehand to chair each group and it was down to each individual to decide which discussion to join. Some were willing to take part in more than one group and this flexibility meant that there were sufficient numbers for each conversation.

The sheets were divided into four main sections: (1) Area of Development; (2) Suggestions; (3) Action; and (4) Who.

The Area of Development started with a shared Summary of the Priority:

'Spirituality' has been defined in different ways over time but it is closely associated with ideas of holiness and life in the Spirit. In the process of Natural Church Development (NCD) it is particularly linked to: (1) The Church; (2) Prayer; (3) The Bible; (4) Lived experience of God. In our survey we scored well on our passion for the Church (1) but not so well on the subsequent elements.

This was followed by a sentence focusing on each of the areas under consideration:

- This discussion is centred on improving how we speak to God in the prayer life of St Mary's.
- This discussion is centred on improving how we read the Bible in the spiritual life of St Mary's.
- This discussion is centred on improving our lived experience of God in St Mary's.

This section also included a date for completion of any action points, which was the same for each group.

The second section set out to explore specific suggestions and ideas. This included those that had come through the cards given out during the sermons as well as any proposals that members of the group had for discussion. The next section asked the group to decide upon up to three action points to take forward. They could choose just one or two actions: the reason for putting an upper limit was to keep the process manageable.

The final section looked at who would implement these ideas, including 'responsibilities for implementation', 'timescales and deadlines', 'resources' and 'recommendations for on-going action'. The thinking behind this was about ownership of the suggestions. The standing committee felt that if the proposals were taken forward by the church as a whole there was a greater chance of them putting down roots and becoming embedded in church life. These were completed, although one group needed a follow-up meeting to finish the task.

At this point in the story, the minister did something against the advice of the church's NCD mentor which had been shared at the start of the cycle. At the start of May he went on a period of sabbatical study leave, which included carrying out some of the research into the forms of organizational narrative found in churches set out in previous chapters. However, this is where the collaborative approach taken by the group overseeing the process proved invaluable. Leadership of this project was not dependent on one individual and the conveners of the groups with responsibility for each area of development were able to take forward their action points.

Arriving at outcomes

In July a summary document was produced for the church by the standing committee to show how the agreed action points had been implemented. These included:

Prayer action points:

1 To develop an area within the church that is available at all times for quiet prayer and is not part of the tourist trail.
2 Prayer of the week/month to be published in the Newsletter.
3 Prayer Group to be set up.

Bible-reading action points

1 Towards raising the profile of the Bibles that are available in church, there is now a poster on the hymnbook case at the back of church, drawing attention to the Bibles on the bottom shelf.

Extra Bibles have been added, though the total number has since decreased, so we will be asking congregation members if they have any spare copies of the Bible they could donate. In addition, we may buy specific translations in due course, to broaden the range of versions on offer.

2 As a first step to raising the profile of regular Bible-reading with the congregation, the Bible references for the following week's readings now appear in the weekly Newsletter.

3 A medium-term aim – to raise the profile of the Bible with our young church (Family Services & Sunday School) – was suggested. The 'Bible' group will meet again in September to explore how we might develop this, and other ideas.

Lived experience of God action points

1 Canon David Pettifor preached on the subject of Mindfulness and the Christian Faith, in St Mary's on Sunday 28th June.

2 Organize a series of coffee meetings to give an opportunity for members of the congregation to meet in an informal way, to take time out from the everyday routines of life to reflect and consider God's presence in our lives. (And perhaps give the opportunity if someone wanted to, for them to share these with others.) Initial thoughts: fortnightly, Thursday at 9.30 am in the Vestry.

3 Establish who would be interested in attending a similar group to the one above, but at a Breakfast meeting on a Saturday morning, monthly or bi-monthly, so that there is accessibility for those working during the week. Paul and Catherine Watkins are exploring this.

The church had now completed the six stages of the NCD cycle: (1) Testing – introducing the survey and carrying it out; (2) Understanding – analysing the data and deciding which elements needed addressing; (3) Planning – drawing up a response via sermons and church discussions; (4) Doing – carrying through that response; (5) Experiencing – embedding the groups and actions; and (6) Perceiving.

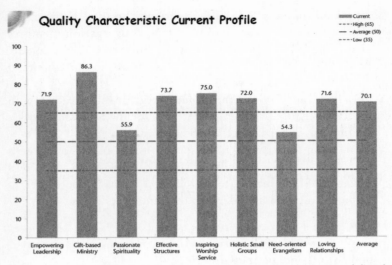

Images from the results of the second NCD survey of St Mary's, Warwick (2016)

Figure 6: Quality Characteristic Current Profile handout from NCD Status Guide (January 2016).

A second survey was undertaken in January 2016 which provided some indications of how this work had impacted upon the Passionate Spirituality indicator at St Mary's. In terms of the measured indicators it had not only risen but was also no longer the lowest stave on the barrel (see Figure 6).

Analysing St Mary's NCD Story

We turn from the account of how the first cycle of the NCD programme was implemented to explore how the St Mary's NCD story maps on to the ideas we have considered in previous chapters about narrative ecology, forms of church storytelling and curating stories in churches. In addition to the story we shall also examine the language and some of the contradictions that we identify as inherent in the NCD approach.

Narrative ecologies

As we discussed at the beginning of this chapter, one of the key organizational metaphors for the NCD programme is growth and nurture. This image implies change and development, but how that comes about and what form it takes will depend on how the cycle is implemented. In our chapter on 'Living in multiple stories' we set out Gabriel's ideas about narrative ecology and we can return to those now and examine how the narrative ecology in a process like NCD will depend on how it is led. For example, it could be led in a way that treats the cycle like a narrative monoculture: that is to say, the meta-story of how the programme will work in the local environment, together with the eight individual stories around each category, are what Gabriel calls 'hegemonic narratives' to which all stories have to conform and few (if any) counter-stories are permitted.

An approach like NCD could also be led in the form of narrative allotments. Once again the meta-story of the NCD cycle is a carefully tended plot in which the stories for each of the eight categories are also cultivated with certain interests in mind. These interests might be internal to a church and have regard to particularly powerful individuals or groups, but the stories might also have external concerns in mind – is external funding or advancement in the wider church dependent on a neat, thriving allotment?

By contrast, in some ecclesiologies local churches can have a great deal of independence so it is hard for those charged with managing such a group to impose their narrative upon it. They may try to do so but the power of local stories and storytellers means that it is difficult for stories from outside to get any hold or purchase in the community. In that case even a programme like NCD can risk becoming bogged down in narrative marshlands, particularly if those leading the process are unable to see a way forward.

NCD ecologies

Where does this account of one church's NCD cycle stand in terms of a narrative ecology, and has the way it was led cultivated both the environment and the way in which stories were grown? There is a sense in which this programme is clearly controlling or hegemonic. On the one hand, within the Diocese of Coventry no church or minister was compelled to undertake NCD; but, on the other hand, if you wished to be a training incumbent with responsibility for a curate or have any form of paid diocesan support in your locality then you had to have engaged with the NCD process. Furthermore, when a vicar moves on or retires then the appointment of a replacement can only be done through this programme – no NCD survey: no new minister.

In addition, the language used in the surveys comes from a certain section of the Church. Although the programme has been used across the spectrum of church traditions (including Orthodoxy) it reflects terminology and vocabulary which is much more common on the Evangelical wing of that spectrum. Thus, not only does it influence the way in which stories are told and shared, together with the theological and pastoral lexicon that has to be used, but there is also no flexibility in the questions and what they ask. The process takes little account of local climate or narrative diversity.

The way in which the NCD process was implemented at St Mary's aimed at providing as much theological and narrative openness as possible within the limitations of the programme. To a certain extent the language and the structure was non-negotiable, but how it was implemented meant there was space for people to share their ideas. We shall examine that in more detail when we look at how stories were curated through that first NCD cycle, but before we discuss that we shall explore how this account of St Mary's experience relates to the interpretive, identity and improvised stories outlined in previous chapters.

Narrative forms

Interpretive stories

The interpretive stories identified previously were: (1) Theological narratives; (2) Ecclesial narratives; and (3) Liturgical narratives, and we can make some brief comments under each of these headings.

Theological narratives   Given that the research into NCD has been undertaken by someone described as a 'theologian' there is remarkably little theological underpinning in Schwarz's research and analysis. The most significant ideas are the language of growth and images of the vine and body. In an introduction to his approach Schwarz writes about how he presents his programme to new enquirers who come to meet him: 'I try to give them a biblically-based paradigm – an alternate way of looking at things, usually in the form of a story, a picture, or a diagram – and then I ask questions and let my visitors reflect on them' (Schwarz, 2015, p. 7).

Most often, however, these tend not to be biblical or theological. The lowest stave of the barrel is a good example (Figure 5). Another picture that Schwarz uses is the image of two men clearly struggling to propel a cart with square wheels (Figure 7). The wagon itself is carrying round wheels and is then contrasted with the cart when 'the round wheels have been put in their proper place' (Schwarz, 2015, pp. 15 and 18). The two men struggling with the wagon that had square wheels are suddenly mobile and moving freely when the correct tools for the task are being employed.

These are striking images but hardly theological or biblical, and they take us back to our earlier comments about the curious mixture of language in the NCD approach. The approach here is entirely functional and pragmatic. It is not related in any way to theological insight or biblical story. Equally, there is nothing in organizational theory which would lead us to expect that such a mechanistic approach is likely to be helpful in strengthening the organization. Diagnostics that help an organization to reflect on where it is in its own story have always had a place, but with caveats saying that they give a language for debate, not a measure to aspire to.

Ecclesial narratives   A handbook was written by NCD to launch this initiative in the Diocese of Coventry for 2013, and the slightly updated 2015 version is available on the diocesan website here: www.dioceseofcoventry.org/images/document_library /UDR00062.pdf. Throughout the document there is a tension

Figure 7: Carts with square and round wheels.

between the language of a *healthy* church and a *growing* church. For instance, under the heading 'Thinking Growth . . . Naturally' the handbook states:

> Scripture teaches that the local church is also a living organism which God wants to grow – the Body of Christ. The local church shares similarities with other organisms God has created and sustains. Its potential for growth lies in its health, not its size. NCD has demonstrated decisively through comprehensive international research that healthy growing churches are more

successful in releasing the potential for healthy growth because they apply these natural principles and treat the church more as a living organism to be grown rather than an organization to be built. (*Introductory Handbook*, 2015, p. 8)

A vital image in this process is Jesus' story of the growing seed, where Jesus says:

> This is what the Kingdom of God is like. A farmer scatters seed on the ground. Night and day, whether he sleeps or gets up, the seed sprouts and grows, though he does not know why. All by itself the soil produces grain – first the stalk, then the head, then the full kernel in the head. As soon as the grain is ripe, he puts the sickle to it, because the harvest has come. (Mark 4.26–29)

The principal lesson the NCD handbook draws from Jesus' parable is that growth is a co-operative effort. On the one hand the farmer creates an environment which maximizes the potential for new life and growth by consistently removing the obstacles to healthy growth. On the other hand, God alone brings that life and growth – which appears to happen 'all by itself' to the farmer (*Introductory Handbook*, 2015, p. 8). Throughout the programme the dominant ecclesial narrative is one of growth. If churches are healthy they will be growing, so if they are not growing they cannot be healthy.

To this end the language of many questions in the NCD process are located within a specific ecclesial narrative – that which sees the role of local churches to be growing organizations. The implication is that this growth will be numerical. Although from the outset the handbook stresses that quality is the basis for church growth, it is clear that quantity will be the signifier that there is quality. However, there are numerous other stories and metaphors in Jesus' teaching which could be used to develop alternative ecclesial narratives (for example, 'kingdom', 'foundation', 'servant', 'prophet', 'salt', 'yeast' and more). Yet these are not considered in either practical or theological terms by the NCD approach. We shall explore these in more detail when we look at the improvised narratives.

Liturgical narratives The greater part of St Mary's exploration of its first NCD cycle took place within the context of worship and, in particular, services of Holy Communion and Choral Eucharist. These provided the contexts for the sermons introducing the programme as a whole and then the survey itself. They were also, in the first instance, the setting in which the church community as a whole was invited to respond to the 8 Essential Qualities. Significantly, although there are questions in the survey about sermons (Q10 and Q25 under Worship), music (Q53) and whether worship is inspiring (Q47), there is no mention whatsoever of the Eucharist or Holy Communion in the questionnaire or the diocesan *Introductory Handbook*. This is clearly a serious omission for churches that see their own narrative story in terms of the story about Jesus breaking bread with his followers on the night before his betrayal and death.

Identity stories

The identity stories we considered in Chapter 3 were: (1) Historical narratives; (2) Organizational narratives; and (3) Personal narratives. However, a sense of identity and stories about identity do not play much part in the NCD process. There are no questions in the survey about historical or personal identity, although we argue that there is an implicit sense of organizational identity. There is one statement about identity in the *Introductory Handbook* under the negative heading 'What NCD is not': 'NCD is not a substitute for a church finding its own sense of identity and direction. NCD cannot be "the vision" but it does help clarify and stimulate that sense of identity and direction' (*Introductory Handbook*, 2015, p. 7).

The omission of any discussion about identity is fundamental, in that it excludes the specific narratives that churches, communities and individuals tell about themselves. It could be argued that considering the unique identity stories of each church would be beyond the scope of the NCD process, but there is a deeper issue at stake. The NCD handbook for Coventry Diocese makes the case that, on the basis of their research, 'there are indeed universal God-given principles that can be applied to the unique issues in every local church' (*Introductory Handbook*, 2015, p. 10). That is a big claim to make and, we would argue, goes beyond the evidence provided. In fact, there could never be sufficient data to substantiate such an assertion.

Improvised stories

The nine improvised stories outlined in Chapter 8 were: (1) Finance, (2) Architecture, (3) Governance, (4) Pastoral, (5) Mission, (6) Education, (7) Media, (8) Artistic, (9) Untended stories. The five of these that occur most often in the survey questions are: (3) Governance, (5) Mission, (6) Education, and (9) Untended stories. Having said that, those stories that the survey questions do not explore are equally significant.

1 *Finance* – It is surprising that neither the NCD handbook nor the questionnaire makes any mention of church accounts or finances. The stories told about money and resources are a good indication of power and priorities in a church. We can see something of this in the quote from one of Vaughan's sermons introducing the survey, where the NCD programme was a precursor in St Mary's for a stewardship campaign.
2 *Architecture* – The only reference to buildings in the NCD handbook is to urge that the construction of new facilities should not be allowed to delay undertaking the survey (*Introductory Handbook*, 2015, p. 16). We know that the internal form of a church building and stories about how it came into being can all shape important elements of ongoing congregational narrative.
3 *Governance* – There are many questions in the survey about governance, including two categories that major on data and stories under the headings Empowering Leadership and Effective Structures. There are also questions under Holistic Small Groups (Q76 The leaders of our small groups are trained for their tasks) and Need-oriented Evangelism (Q82 The leaders of our church support individual Christians in their evangelistic endeavours) which touch on this. Governance is clearly a key element in the NCD programme.

4 *Pastoral* – The story of pastoral care emerges in various questions across the different characteristics. For instance, under the heading Holistic Small Groups, Q49 asks for a response to the statement: I am a member of a group in our church where it is possible to talk about personal problems. The potential for this narrative to appear most clearly is within the profile for Loving Relationships, where over half the questions invite respondents to think about how aspects of church life are told or shared in conversation with others.

5 *Mission* – This is another principal concern and there are many questions about mission under the categories of Need-orientated Evangelism and Holistic Small Groups. The emphasis on each church's missional story is also present in Worship (Q85 Our worship service attracts unchurched visitors) and Empowering Leadership (Q22 Our leaders are clearly concerned for people who do not know Jesus Christ).

6 *Education* – Although there is not a single category that addresses the stories told about education, there are questions about training and supervision for congregational members across several of the NCD factors – for example, under Empowering Leadership (Q81 Our leaders regularly receive assistance from an outside person on how to develop our church) and under Gift-based Ministry (Q58 The volunteers of our church are trained for their ministries).

7 *Media* – There do not appear to be any questions that deal with regular or social media, and how churches tell their stories to local communities and the outside world.

8 *Art* – There is also very little attempt to elicit stories around creative arts and music. In the NCD handbook making music is seen as an example of a Holistic Small Group (*Introductory Handbook*, 2015, p. 18). In the survey itself one question under Inspiring Worship asks for a response to the statement: The music in the worship service helps me worship God (Q53). Otherwise questions and stories about art and music are largely absent.

9 *Untended Stories* – Interestingly, across three of the categories there are four questions that touch on potentially unresolved problems and stories of conflicts in a church: Q30 In our church

it is possible to talk with other people about personal problems; Q49 I am a member of a group in our church where it is possible to talk about personal problems; Q61 Our leaders show concern for the personal problems of those in ministry; Q80 If I have a disagreement with a member of our church, I will go to them in order to resolve it. Although the NCD programme would not put it in these terms, there is a willingness within the survey to address some narratives that might otherwise be untold.

Thus far in this section of the chapter we have explored the narrative ecology of the NCD programme at St Mary's and mapped the first cycle of the 8EQs on to the different forms of interpretive, identity and improvised story. In his critique of McDonaldization and managerialism in churches Drane observes that story has 'become a primary vehicle for meaning' (Drane, 2000, p. 140), and notes how even an organization as wedded to the 'iron cage of efficiency' as McDonald's tells a powerful story, which has been a crucial part of its success (p. 153). The NCD programme touches on some of the forms of church story that we have identified, but not in any self-conscious or thoroughgoing way that might lead to an understanding of how narratives work or might be curated. It is to that aspect we now turn.

Curating the narratives

In Chapter 5 we explored the notion of curating stories in organizations and churches, so under this heading we shall now return to the five practical ways described there in which narratives can be nurtured and cultivated within the context of a managerial approach such as NCD.

Leaders need to be aware of stories circulating

The story of NCD in the Diocese of Coventry began in 2006/7 when the Warwick and Leamington deanery began exploring the programme under the leadership of the then area dean, who was eager to establish a shared plan for all the churches in the deanery and encouraged each church to undertake an NCD survey in order to assist in this process. Vaughan recalls his own initial response as having fundamental doubts about the viability of this approach. Parish churches are notably independent in their theological outlooks, their finances and their storytelling. Truth be told, he expected the process to be like a firework – exploding with much light and sound, before fading into the night. Nevertheless, St Mary's undertook a survey in the expectation of its minister that it would yield little and the process would pass.

In 2009 the new Bishop of Coventry, Christopher Cocksworth, set out his vision for the diocese in the document *Signposts for the Future*.[7] Interestingly, he makes some references to the importance of story – most especially in discussing Coventry Cathedral:

> One of the reasons for 'the strong bonds of mutuality that exist' has been our Cathedral's story of reconciliation which historically has influenced the character of the Diocese over the years. I have been surprised in my travels by how little the theme of reconciliation has been explicitly raised, apart from in our schools. (*Signposts for the Future*, 2009, p. 19)[8]

Although there is much discussion of mission, the vision made no reference to NCD or to growing healthy churches. The closest it comes is a statement about mission action plans: 'Some Dioceses, for example, ask all their communities, and in some cases whole Deaneries, to devise Mission Action Plans. We could do the same in terms of local application of our overall purposes. That's something to think about' (*Signposts for the Future*, 2009, p. 5).

In 2010 the area dean became archdeacon with responsibility for encouraging mission in Coventry Diocese, and as part of that brief he began rolling the NCD programme out across the diocese. It became clear to clergy and churches that there was to be no escape from the NCD approach, although there was some advantage to those churches in Warwick and Leamington in that this process had already started to become part of their stories.

Leaders can modify negative stories

Is the introduction of NCD into the diocese a negative story? Anecdotal experience from two churches in the Warwick Team illustrates clearly how the answer to this is mixed. On the one hand, the team vicar of a relatively small church with an evangelical ethos that is in tune with the theological language of NCD has reported a number of times how undertaking the surveys has given that church a much clearer sense of direction. On the other hand, members from Warwick's most Anglo-Catholic parish, who had to undertake the survey in order to appoint a new priest, recounted how the language of leadership, particularly under the Empowering Leadership category, made it much harder for their more priestly understanding of ministry to be heard.

We have seen in the account of St Mary's first NCD cycle that, despite some misgivings, in his sermons Vaughan sought to frame the process and results in a way that he felt would be helpful and positive. For instance, he outlined what he felt were some of the advantages of the programme (it did not see itself as a 'silver bullet'; it is a tool to be used and not a cage to imprison; the language was about quality and not quantity). In addition, although the programme requires churches to focus on their weakest category he also emphasized the results from St Mary's stronger categories. And he encouraged the church to reflect critically upon the language and the process.

Additionally and more importantly, the story was modified through the way in which the NCD cycle was introduced and the whole church encouraged to participate and input into the discussion. Although a select group of 30 people was chosen for the survey, the wider church community was encouraged to take part through the cards given out in services for comments, the sermons about NCD being available online and in printed format so that people could catch up and comment, and the process of discussing how to take matters forward being open to anyone who wished to be involved. By spreading the leadership of the process along with the involvement of the church as widely as possible, the next chapter in the story could be written, modified and owned by a broad group in St Mary's.

People are empowered if they can contribute to the story

As this minute from St Mary's church council makes clear, those leading the response to the survey believed that the wider church should be contributing to the next stage of the story:

> Standing Committee felt it was important that the whole church should be involved in reflecting and acting on this, so to this end Vaughan would be preaching a series of 4 sermons addressing the positives and negatives that came out of the review and seeking congregational suggestions for actions. The sermons would be placed on the website and paper copies at the back of church. The feedback would be followed by a discussion and lunch on 18th April, to discuss the way forward and agree on further action points. (PCC minutes, 21 January 2015)

This inclusive approach to the NCD cycle empowered a number of people to engage with leadership at St Mary's in new ways; and it picks up an idea we discussed in Chapter 2, that stories are a good way to 'see what God is doing and join in' and to allow people to be significant voices in their own story. The three groups looking at the issues of prayer, Bible study and lived experience of God were specifically asked to identify 'responsibilities for implementation'. It was also made clear that it was not expected that the task of taking proposals forward would fall on the standing committee. Furthermore, the vicar was not going to be around during the period for the realization of ideas as he would be on sabbatical study leave. David has observed that the requirement for the vicar to remain for the whole process indicates a particular view of leadership being vested in *one* leader.

The outcome from the discussions and implementation has been set out above (page 158) under the heading *Arriving at outcomes* and the list of action points taken forward under the three sub-headings of Prayer, Bible reading and Lived experience of God.

Leaders need to know that all their actions can become stories

When did this story begin? It could be argued that it started when an area dean encouraged the Warwick and Leamington deanery to engage in the NCD programme, or when he subsequently became archdeacon and rolled the process out across Coventry Diocese. Those actions have started many stories. More recently the Bishop of Coventry has described the eight NCD qualities as 'ecclesial virtues' which 'seek to form the church communities into a fuller ecclesial reality, generating growth'. Although he does not mention story in his analysis, he is aware that this is a work in progress and the narrative is ongoing:

> Space does not allow for a more thorough analysis of how this pattern of church life is strategically applied, resourced and then scrutinized in a diocese. We ourselves are in the early stages of doing so, and I am hesitant to make too many claims about its outcomes. (Cocksworth, 2015, p. 83)

In terms of the specific story being explored here, that of St Mary's engagement with NCD, we know that the vicar was not an enthusiastic proponent of the approach but came to the conclusion it had to be undertaken and the only way to modify the story was to engage with it and for the church to begin writing its own chapters. That decision meant from 5th September 2013, the NCD process began to shape the story of the church as it enters the official minutes of the standing committee for the first time and the diocesan handbook was given out for people to read. From that point onwards, the actions of the standing committee and all who contributed to the leadership of this process became part of the story of NCD at St Mary's.

Recognize this is not univocal

Who are the different voices involved in telling this story, how many are speaking, and are they in harmony or at cross-purposes? We can see three conversational partners in the narrative presented by this chapter. These are the NCD voice, the diocesan voices and the local voices. We shall look briefly, in turn, at the contribution of each.

First, Christian Schwarz, the NCD team and the voices that are reflected in the process itself. Their narrative comes through most clearly in the survey questions and Schwarz's book *The All By Itself Anglican* (2015). The NCD programme does make some limited acknowledgement of variety in its narrative for healthy churches. For instance, we can see the eight categories as some recognition of a multivalent approach. However, there is a limit to this breadth of narrative voice.

For example, Schwarz tells the story of how he was once asked by Donald McGavran, the father of the Church Growth Movement, 'What is the true fruit of an apple tree?' Schwarz replied, 'It's an apple, of course.' Then McGavran said, 'You're wrong. The true fruit of an apple tree is not an apple, but another apple tree.' Schwarz continues:

> [T]he true fruit of a small group is not a new Christian, but another group; and the true fruit of an evangelist is not a convert, but new evangelists; and the true fruit of a church is not a new group, but another church; and the true fruit of a leader is not followers, but new leaders. (Schwarz, 2015, pp. 90–1)

It is difficult to escape the idea that the kind of growth Schwarz is seeking is a simple reproduction, which is very different from Jesus' parable about the mustard seed, for instance (Luke 13.18–19). He further illustrates the story of McGavran's apple tree with the example of waterlilies covering a pond. It is far from clear what place other forms of fruit, water plants or models of discipleship might have in Schwarz's narrative ecology.

A second collection of voices in this story is that of Coventry Diocese, which emerges through individuals commending the NCD programme (such as bishops, archdeacons, NCD mentors and other churches) but most especially in the *Introductory Handbook*. Once again there is some affirmation of diversity – for example, a statement in the diocesan handbook outlines how the survey results will be fed back in a variety of forms:

- The Summary Guide offers a short overview of the results.
- The Story Guide views the results from a thematic perspective, that is, the results for individual NCD Survey questions are grouped under pre-determined themes.
- The Status Guide offers a comprehensive question-by-question analysis of the results.
- The Strategy Guide invites consideration of future outcomes if present health issues in the life of the church are addressed. (*Introductory Handbook*, 2015, p. 19)

Furthermore the handbook is clear that each church will face its own particular challenges: 'Your church is unique and every time you get your Survey results, it will be facing a unique set of health issues (*Introductory Handbook*, 2015, p. 20). In other words, there should be (potentially at least) many different ways to implement change and tell stories about that process. Having said that, we have already noted that the language of NCD and its underlying ecclesiology only allow for different voices and vocabulary up to a point.

Another community of voices in the story is provided by St Mary's church. We've drawn attention to this throughout the chapter – particularly the widespread participation that was encouraged throughout the NCD cycle. We noted that this was the case from very early on in the process and it was carried on through to the implementation of the action points.

The final voices are those of the narrators. Much of this has been provided by Vaughan but David has made inputs to this narrative as well. Geoff Mead writes about leading as being less about taking charge and making things happen and more about participating in a social process of making sense of things. He tells a wonderful story about a group of anthropologists searching for rock paintings:

Some years ago, a group of Bushmen agreed to lead a party of anthropologists into the Kalahari to see some ancient rock paintings that were rumoured to be found deep in the desert. After two weeks, travelling through the sandy wastes, they came to an escarpment and the Bushmen announced that they had arrived. The anthropologists took out their equipment and scoured the sacred site. They peeked and peered, they brushed and scraped but found nothing, not a single painting. After a while they gave up, complaining that they had been brought to the wrong place. The Bushmen laughed and went up to the same spot that the anthropologists had so closely examined; they unstoppered the gourds of water they had with them and splashed the contents over the sun-bleached surface of the rock. Dozens of dazzling colored images – women, children, hunters, eland, kudu, wildebeest, and lions – sprang from the rock and burst into life. (Mead, 2014, pp. 10–11)

If we apply Mead's parable to the process of leading in the NCD programme, we argue that it is not about getting the right results or correct outcomes from a quantitative survey. Instead it is about helping a community to splash water on to a rock and discover what is already there. There are numerous stories being told just as there were many images on the rocks. By being open to a variety of storytelling forms and a diverse narrative ecology, which encourages a range of voices to curate the stories, the NCD process can be opened into something that does encounter and engage with the needs and conversations of local communities.

Summary and conclusion

This chapter has been a case study in narrative leadership for a local church but within a context that has strong traits of managerialist culture. We began by noting Parker's three strands of this regulative approach: control over nature, control over humans and control over organizational abilities or technologies. There is a clear tension at work in the NCD programme because, while it makes a claim that healthy growth is 'all by itself', we can also see those three aspects of control at work in the process.

We have told the story of how one particular church undertook the first cycle of what are called the 8 Essential Qualities for a healthy church. This included hearing some of the narrative that Vaughan shared in his sermons on how the process could be framed, and the story he told as he reported back the results from the church's quantitative survey. Two crucial elements in this were: (1) keeping the story open for as many participants as possible; and (2) sharing the leadership of how the narrative was to develop without pre-conditions to the ending. The outcome was that three key areas for development were identified and an open meeting was convened to discuss how they might be addressed. Action points were identified and taken forward, and a summary was produced to show how they had been implemented. A further survey was undertaken showing a rise across the eight categories.

While we agree that there were some results from the NCD process, we would argue that they were achieved in large part because the NCD garment was carefully adapted and tailored to local needs. In that respect, when it came to mapping the story on to Gabriel's narrative ecology it could be treated as a temperate climate, rather than as a marshland or monoculture where stories get bogged down or are uniform.

However, when it came to our interpretive, identity and improvised forms of narrative, we found that there were some serious omissions in the NCD process. At one level it claims to stress the importance of Scripture and biblical images, but when it comes to engaging with a church's culture and stories the focus switches to non-biblical images such as a barrel or a cart with square wheels. There are several stories that are invisible to the NCD survey, including vital liturgical stories such as the Last Supper (Holy Communion), identity stories such as a local church's own history, and improvised stories where finance, architecture and media are absent. This does raise a serious question about the scope of the questionnaire and the quality of data that is collated. Stories have to be heard for any good to come of them. If you are given a checklist of statements to rate about an individual church, such as NCD gives you, and a form of analysis for the answers, your chances of actually listening to the stories being told in your church, hearing them and building on them, are reduced. NCD, like other ways of mechanizing listening, is likely to be good at surveying attitudes to particular statements, but this does not enable you to hear, under-stand, or lead the stories, which are always much more holistic.

Finally, we examined how stories were curated during the cycle and how leaders need to be aware of stories circulating and are able to modify negative stories; how people are empowered if they can contribute to the story; how leaders need to know that all their actions can become stories; and how they should recognize that storytelling and story sharing in churches is not univocal. We shall now turn, in our final chapter, to explore some specific ideas on how to lead stories in churches.

Questions

1 What kind of 'tick box' environments have you worked in with churches?
2 Were there conflicting metaphors being used to describe that nar-rative ecology? If so, what were they?
3 What kinds of story were being curated and how did they work together or diverge?

Notes

1 www.dioceseofcoventry.org/UnderstandingChurchHealth, accessed 27.2.2017.
2 www.dioceseofcoventry.org/UnderstandingChurchHealth/healthy churchesstrategy, accessed 27.2.2017.
3 www.dioceseofcoventry.org/UnderstandingChurchHealth/healthy churchesstrategy, accessed 27.2.2017.
4 A version of the St Mary's Story was presented to a diocesan NCD mentors' meeting in Coventry on 22 March 2017.
5 The full sermon can be found on the church's website here: www .stmaryswarwick.org.uk/images/uploads/2014_sermon_2Before_Advent _8_Qualities.pdf, accessed 27.2.2017.
6 Further details of the National College for Teaching and Leadership's *Leading and Managing Change* module can be found here: www.national college.org.uk/transfer/open/dsbm-phase-4-module-2-leading-and-manag ing-change/making-change-happen/change-teams.html, accessed 20.3.2017.

7 Available on the diocesan website here: www.dioceseofcoventry.org /images/document_library/UDR00306.pdf, accessed 2.2.2017.

8 See also footnote 18 on the same page which reads: 'A *story* that is movingly told by Stephen Verney in his *Fire in Coventry* to be reprinted for the Jubilee celebrations, and in Brian Frost's *biography* of Marjorie Milne, a remarkable woman who arrived in the city of Coventry in 1958 believing that God had sent her to the city to wait in prayer because he was about to do a new work (see Brian Frost, *Glastonbury Journey*)' (our emphasis).

Conclusion: Ten Ideas for Leading by Story in Churches

In the preceding chapters we have discussed many features of why stories matter in organizations, and we have discussed how stories work and what they can do. In this chapter we will offer some specific practical suggestions on how to be effective in leading by story in churches. As in the rest of the book, we are talking about all who are involved in leading within the church, not only about ordained ministers. Leadership, when done well, requires contributions from many different people, and it works best when the appropriate person steps forward to lead at a particular time, and then steps back to enable someone else to step forward and lead. Our image is rather like the way a team member in football or rugby will do something with the ball and then choose the moment to pass it to someone else. Leadership is best when it is passed around, with each person keeping it for long enough to do something with it, but no one holding on to it for too long, which can be selfish and ineffective. If you don't relate to that image, leadership is rather like a chamber choir[1] where each member will make their contribution and will occasionally sing solos, but most of the time the audience should not know exactly which contribution is coming from whom. If you can pick out the individual voice, that is dominance rather than leadership, and not good for the performance as a whole. All the members are involved in leadership, not just the conductor, and all are skilled at being influenced by the other voices, or in other words accepting leadership. Similarly, this book is not just for ordained ministers, but for all who are involved in enabling something to happen in churches which was not going to happen otherwise, including treasurers, musicians, house group leaders, caterers, flower arrangers and so on all round the church.

In offering a narrative understanding of leadership in churches, we are not saying that here, at last, is the true understanding of how to lead. The field has been bedevilled by too many offerings that purport to give the answer, or more of the answer than anything else to date, as to how leadership can best be thought of. Instead, we offer the notion of leading by story, not as the only answer or even always the best answer on how to lead, but as a contribution to the menu of ideas and options that you bring with you to situations in which you wish to lead or to support leadership.

We have talked about what it means to lead by story through the previous chapters and we shall take ideas and conclusions from those chapters as read, without referring back to them exhaustively. In this chapter we want to conclude by offering ten practical ideas for putting some of these ideas into practice.

1 Know your story

Goffee and Jones (2006) say that a key quality in leadership is to be yourself but more so. Identity has come up several times in this book, and is inseparable from storytelling. Our characters and identities are in the stories that we tell and that are told about us. Stories are filled with characters who are actors in the story, and we will inevitably appear as characters in the stories we tell. Some have even argued that the meaning of life is to appear in the stories of others. It is one of the most natural ways in which people disclose something of themselves. How do I cast myself in my own stories and how do I wish to appear in the stories of others? How do I maintain some consistency and coherence in my own story while appearing in the stories of others? If you lose track of your own story, this seems to us to be very similar to the idea of 'losing your own soul'. To work well with you, others need to know what you are about, where your story has come from and where it is going. This requires a degree of consistency in your story, or people do not know who they are dealing with. It also requires a degree of inconsistency, of signs of growth and change, some kind of narrative arc. The totally consistent person is not very credible and too boring to be an interesting participant in the stories of others. When we talk about the storied nature of life in organizations, we may expect the people who have parts in our story to be interesting, to surprise us on occasions.

Most of us lose the plot sometimes. We become bored with our own story, or we forget why we got involved in some activity in the first place. These are dangerous moments. In our life stories, this is when we undergo a mid-life crisis as we seek to do something, anything, to liven up our stories. These are times when we can destroy a story that we may have spent years building up. We are not meaning to decry people leading exciting lives, but rather to point out that there is a lot of value personally in being aware of where we are in our own story, and who we are wanting to become through it. This story then also needs to link with the role that you are playing in the leading that you do in the church. How does what Chris, over there, is doing fit into her view of her own story and the church's story? If I cannot answer that question I will probably find it more difficult to trust Chris to act consistently and to build up her story in a way that makes sense to me.

MacIntyre (1981) says: 'I can only answer the question "What am I to do?" if I can answer the prior question "Of what story or stories do I find myself a part?"' (p. 216). Our actions are developments of the plot in our own story and in the stories of others around us. They have implications for the extent to which others can flourish, particularly if we have not noticed that our story line for what is going on is quite different from theirs. If we see ourselves as engaged in a heroic rescue, but others see us as an interfering busybody, this is not likely to end well. We need to be aware both of our own story, and of how the guest appearance we have just made in someone else's story plays out within that story. We have to be alert to hearing their version of their story, even as we are acting within our own. This precludes us from indulging in the feeling that is sometimes (mis)-labelled as 'strong leadership', where we act decisively without taking the trouble to find out how we are appearing in the stories of others.

2 Know the story of Christianity

All churches tell stories about Christianity, about the gospel, about the meaning of their faith and about the relationship with God and with each other that is implicit in this. Most churches favour some forms of storytelling over others. Some will favour a eucharistic approach, where the story of salvation is told and retold regularly through the sacrament of Holy Communion. Some will favour a way of telling the story of Christianity as it can be seen in the lives of members of their congregation, for example through the giving of testimonies, which are stories that a person tells of their relationship with God. Others will favour a story of Christianity that emphasizes the intervention of the Holy Spirit. Even when a church favours long sermons with many words, perhaps including a few illustrative stories, there is usually also an overall story being told about Christianity, for example, about the importance of personal faith. So there are different ways in which the story will be told in different churches, but in most cases we will find ourselves responding to the authority of someone who knows well the story that they want to tell. By the nature of their church roles, David listens to a lot more sermons than Vaughan, and is grateful for the many times when a preacher has clearly studied the Bible long and hard, and then thought and challenged themselves equally hard, to become very clear about the story they are telling. It really shows, and it really increases the trust of the listener in the preacher.

Flannery O'Connor (1969) said, 'In the long run, a people is known, not by its statements or its statistics, but by the stories it tells' (p. 192). These will be the intentionally told stories, relayed through the symbolism or the words that are used, and equally the stories that leak out to anyone who has ears to hear them. Does this church generate an air of depression, of lacking direction, of having collectively forgotten what its story of Christianity actually is? Does it suggest a story that the faith it represents is in retreat, and does not relate to the surrounding world? Alternatively, does it appear to have adopted a story that sounds as if it has been designed to be unconvincing, or even morally repugnant? Are the stories that leak out of the church concerned with fiercely contested views about sex? Or are they stories about the abuse of power by those in authority in the church? Or are they stories about a group of people who love mercy, act justly, and walk humbly before their God? Church members often feel they are misrepresented in the stories that are told about them, but, if you do not take steps for your story to be represented as you would wish, you invite neighbours and journalists to come up with a story about you which will be geared as much to entertainment as to telling the truth, and which will be based on their limited understanding.

Different churches also have their own story about how Christianity came to be as it is, their own story of the early Church. For reasons that are often obscure to outsiders, there are many competing stories about how the early Church was organized, many of these stories being thoroughly researched and carefully grounded, which nevertheless come out as quite different stories. These stories are often part of the competitive stance that churches take towards one another, each trying to show that its own way of doing things is the natural continuation of the early Church. Quite why this should mean that they are right and others are wrong is something that baffles the non-member, but it is a long-running competition. For this reason, we think it is important that some of those involved in church leadership should have a grasp of a reasonably non-partisan story of the early Church.

The story of Christianity is often told not from the pulpit, or over coffee, or in the house group, but through music. Hymns and worship songs are often narrative structures giving the story of the faith. Those who sing them find the words coming back into their minds, unbidden, during the following week, and the music helps them to remember the words and the sequence of the story. This is sometimes dignified by the (probably wrongly attributed) quotation from St Augustine that 'he who sings prays twice'. More importantly, he or she who sings seems to take in the words and remember them, with the tune, without challenging their truthfulness as much as would happen with the spoken word. Hendrix (2015) notes how the impact of Martin Luther's hymns far exceeded his sermons or pamphlets (p. 198). There are many well-worn examples of dubious versions of the story of Christianity being preserved in song. The line from 'All things bright and beautiful' about 'The rich man in his castle, the poor man at his gate', for example, seems to accept a social order that many find unacceptable in a presentation of the story of our faith. The lines from 'Once in royal David's city' which say that 'Christian children all must be mild, obedient, good as he' are a blatant example of the use of religion to control child behaviour. We could continue with more contentious examples, but our point is that music is one of the routes by which people in church tell and hear the story of Christianity, and if the music is any good they will remember the words of the story with the music. It is therefore not an innocent decoration. Any song is going to be at most a partial telling of the story of Christianity, and so the choosing of what is sung is an important part of leading a church. The people doing the choosing need to know the story of Christianity well themselves, and be prepared to use that knowledge in choosing the texts that are going to be sung to music.

3 Know the story of your Church

This is very important to some people and not to others, although it is sometimes difficult for those who care about it to own up to this; it is not a fashionable preoccupation at the moment. This may be an area that those involved in leading in churches need to know in order to understand some of the emotion attaching to particular ideas in their church. One of us recently had a conversation with a friend from another denomination in which we said that a particular theological debate seemed less divisive than it used to be, to which the reply was, 'Yes, but people died for it.' A particular principle becomes an important part of the story of a church not because of its place in current thinking, but because people have been prepared to suffer for it in the past. Instances of this are easy to find in, for example, Northern Ireland.

The extent to which people identify with the story of their denomination is something of a mystery. It matters to many congregations that, even if they seem to be in decline, they can see other congregations around them that are declining faster. In some denominations a battle is fought over generations about the future direction of travel for their churches. We could give many examples of this but, as we are both members of the Church of England, let's start from home, where the battle between different stories that express the heart of the Church of England has been fought out ever since the time of Henry VIII. Stories are told to emphasize its Catholic heritage, or its Protestant roots, or its Evangelical tradition, or its liberal past. Each of these groups has sub-groups which can tell stories to show that they are the true centre of the Church of England, and that the future of the church depends on recognizing the foundational importance of the story they represent, and returning to it.

This may sound rather toxic, so why do we think it is good for those involved in church leadership to know the story of their denomination? Most of these stories are helpfully moderated by understanding the context in which they arose, and understanding the reasons why counter-stories with different emphases have also survived. We think it is valuable to have an understanding of some of the breadth of different stories about and within denominations, so that each of those stories can be taken with more qualification, and more humility. The Anglican priest we knew who believed that the world would be saved through plainsong could have been helped by knowing, or having others around him who knew, more of the history of mission!

4 Know the story of your local church

If you want to be trusted in your church, you need to be aware of its story. In St Martin's church the treasurer, who had been baptized there as a child and was now in her 70s, would refer to some people as 'St Martin's people'. This wound the vicar up, because he thought she meant people with a tenure roughly in the order of her own, and he would come back at her and argue that all members of the congregation were 'St Martin's people'. However, one of us found we had been promoted to this honoured company within two or three years of having turned up there, and we realized that the phrase meant something much more like 'the people who get what St Martin's is about, who have understood its story'. The vicar, a kind, sensitive and charismatic person, had missed both the story and how important it was because he had not thought in those terms.

In one sense it is good to know the story of your church so that you know where all the bodies are buried. You know that particular issues which had never seemed to amount to much anywhere else are major signifiers for this congregation. You may be able to avoid wandering into some minefields, and to understand interpersonal dynamics more quickly. David once did a day's team development with the board of directors of a publishing company. It was 2.30 in the afternoon before he realized that the HR director and the marketing director had been divorced from each other about a year earlier. At 3.30, he realized that the HR director and the CEO were sisters. Ever since, he has done his best to get to hear the local stories before he blunders into action. Hearing the story of your local church also shows respect and interest; think of the people who have failed to hear the bits that matter most in your story, who have spent their time looking over your shoulder for the next person to talk to while you were trying to tell them about the events that have been important to you, and you will appreciate the importance of being seen to hear the local story.

Denning (2011a) discusses why Al Gore managed to be such a dull US presidential candidate in 2000 – so dull that he lost to George W. Bush – and yet made such a big splash with his environmental documentary *An Inconvenient Truth* in 2006, and concludes that in 2000 Gore was still making up his mind as to which persona to adopt, and was not himself excited by the story he was telling, both of which issues were solved by 2006. He could not join in with the story fully until he had decided what the most important part of the story was to him, and who he might be in relation to it. Similarly, we suggest, it is difficult to join in effectively with offering leadership in a church until one knows enough about its story to choose which of the various kinds of contribution that one can make would be the most effective in this story. You need to know what story you are joining in order to know what character you can most usefully be.

When listening, it is important to pay attention to stories of the past, the present and the future, and we come on to those three areas next.

5 Listen to the stories told about the past

Stories about the past tell you what matters to people. In a more fluid way than any mission statement or strategic argument, stories about the past reveal what it is that people think is worth talking about. Whether the stories are precisely correct or not is not the point. The important thing is that, if a story is worth telling, that says something about how the teller sees the church. The story about when the church was full is not one that will ever be proved or disproved by a time-travelling camera (and for many churches it never was true; the Victorians built for growth, not simply to accommodate their current congregations). The story about the flourishing youth club is important because you know that the teller is telling you about a sign of health that they may be missing in the present. To check the story by going back and reading the annual reports of the church at the time when this was going on would be to miss the point. One of us recently had a conversation with a past member who had returned for a social occasion in the body of the church. He spoke about how in his time the 'Back Benchers' (church youth group) would turn out late in the evening after such events to put the building back to order. That seemed to be a story that was not just about the 'good old days' but about identity, belonging and affirmation (this is part of church life that I recognize), even though there is no longer a group of back benchers to perform the task.

Stories about the past are sometimes told wistfully, and there may be some important leading to be done in getting involved in the storytelling and seeing if some of those stories can be retold in a way that makes more of a contribution to the present and the future of the church. For example, is it possible to tell the story about the 'back benchers' in a way that celebrates those who are still around from that time, recognizes that social needs are different now, and looks for continuity with something that will work equally well in the present? We know one church where a churchwarden tells stories of his childhood in the church, when he was head chorister and there were large numbers of activities and members of the congregation. His stories strike a strange note because the building does not appear to be physically big enough to contain all that he remembers, but, more importantly, he is revealing his dream, which is to put the clock back and have it all as he remembers it from 50 years ago. The story needs retelling with less nostalgia, which is a current project.

However, stories of the past are very important in making sure that they are not being dishonoured by accident. Churches move on, but they do not do so faithfully or honestly if they deny or denigrate their own past. We need to honour our stories, even if we now want our story to go in a different direction, and even if we now positively repent of our past story! One way that Vaughan has worked with past stories from churches is to create tales about certain physical aspects of the building such as a fallen pinnacle, some graffiti, a historical object or an unusual tree (for example, Roberts, 2002b, 2015). While being theologically grounded, he feels these also help people to get a sense that they are part of an ongoing narrative in a particular place and be able to imagine their own contributions into its history.

6 Listen to the stories being told of the present

If your church tells consistent stories about what is going on in it in the present, you are in trouble. It may be quite a comfortable form of trouble, quite relaxing, not much tension. It is not, however, a normal state for a lively organization. We discussed earlier Linde's (1993) argument that if stories are completely consistent, they are never coherent. Life is just never that dull. We would hope to see continuous contest between different stories about the present because this is the way that members of a community maintain a conversation in which they seek to understand their own identity and purposes. That is how people show that they care. If there is only one story, that is narrative poverty, and it is usually only achieved in successful and absolute authoritarian structures, which always carry the seeds of their own destruction.

A more important question for stories of the present is, do they show energy? Is anyone excited by them? Imagine yourself telling someone else the story of any good relationship. Is everything settled and stable, or does the very act of telling the story fill you with energy, with humour at funny parts of the relationship, with ideas about where the relationship might go next? If it does not, the relationship probably needs attention and needs livening up. Would you always tell the same story of the relationship, or does that vary from day to day and from one audience to another? Again, we would be suspicious of a story showing too great consistency. It suggests too much rehearsal, too little live, current material. The same would apply to relationships within a church. If there is no bubbling cauldron of different, possibly conflicting, certainly unfinished stories, there is something missing in the life of the congregation.

Stories of the present, like stories of the past, tell you something about what people care about. People tell stories because they want to suggest a particular line of thinking, or they want to be seen in a particular way, or because they want to influence the way that others see what is going on, or sometimes simply because they want to try some ideas out. We all tell some experimental stories, because we want to see others' reaction to particular views. Stories can be one of the safer ways of trying out a view of the world, and seeing how others react to that view. They have the advantage that, if it does not go down well, you can easily retreat to the position that 'it was only a story'. Remember that all these variations in the way that people tell stories of the present are still within the assumption that people are telling what they believe to be the truth. We are not talking about the world of spin, or covering our tracks, or anything like that here.

The notion of the 'sacrament of the present moment' has been important for both of us. Vaughan recalls vividly being introduced to the work of Jean-Pierre de Caussade at theological college and David has written about the value of his work in thinking about organizations (Sims, 2015). That sense of being in the present moment and hearing stories in the present also gives us the chance to see if there are any characters missing that might be appropriate for us. What is not happening in these stories that we might be able to offer? One of us joined two different bodies of trustees within a year, and felt in both cases that the stories being told lacked a particular kind of 'critical friend'. There was no one who would listen quietly and intently to the debate and then ask a question that challenged whether the topic being discussed was the right one, or whether the debate needed reformulating. There were plenty of very competent people in different ways within those trustee bodies, but the stories they were telling about their activity lacked this one role which we felt we could play.

7 Listen to stories of the future

We need to explain what we mean by stories of the future, because some organizations, including some churches, are so poor in stories about the future that the concept can get forgotten. David has spent a good proportion of his working life recruiting people to a business school – professors, lecturers, senior administrators, MBA students, PhD students, undergraduates. In most cases these people would have had a choice as to which business school they joined, with plenty of big names vying for their services or their custom. In this case, recruitment becomes a matter of telling a story of the future of the organization you want them to join. If you come here, what sort of school are you joining? What openings will it create for you in the future? How might you change and develop here? The reason these are stories of the future rather than the present is that they are being told about a moving and changing world. The business school will not be the same in six months' time, when they actually join, as it is now. It is in the process of becoming something different and, hopefully, better. Part of this is that the business school will change because they have joined it. They are being invited not just to come and listen to a future story, but to participate in and to join in creating a future story. To restrict oneself to telling stories of the present in these circumstances would not be any more truthful because, when you engage in this future storytelling, you genuinely believe that the story is moving and will continue to move. You are doing your best to tell the story of the future truthfully, but also creatively. Such storytelling operates on the teller as well as on the listeners. It is not only a way of telling people what they are joining if you are successful in recruiting them; it is also an exercise of the imagination on the part of the storyteller. You are imagining a future, telling people about it, and thereby rehearsing the story to tell to others, like your existing colleagues and students, too. Thus the storytelling of the future actually becomes part of creating the future that you are telling stories about.

This is very different from the fixity and lack of fluidity that we find in some stories of the future. Worst of all is if there are no stories of the future, if no one can see anything exciting coming, or if the focus is so firmly on the past and the present that there seems to be no room for the future. But it is not much better if the only stories of the future are to be found in the mission statement, or the strategic plan, or the targets that a church has set itself. These are techniques for turning stories of the future into formulae, for stripping them of most of their most story-like qualities. They are no longer stories. David was very embarrassed when his former university department, Cass Business School, employed a consultancy to summarize 'the Cass story'. What emerged was a document with facts, propositions, intentions and missions, and not a glimmer of a story. No life, no contention, no need for a story to be performed. Those who value stories are sometimes accused of trying to turn everything into a story, but we would refute this accusation. Some things are not stories but just a series of propositions and, confronted with most strategic plans, it is really easy to tell the difference!

In terms of the Church, we can argue that Christianity implies and possibly includes a story about the future. During the course of writing this book Vaughan had a conversation with a group of visitors in church. One declared that she did not believe in God; the other said that she wished she could and that, although she had been to church earlier in her life, she had now drifted away. The conversation ranged over issues of suffering, religious conflict, the nature of Jesus and more, but it was framed by a discussion about life after death and whether there was 'anything more'. As the discussion continued it seemed to Vaughan that the different future stories (heaven or hell, eternal life or oblivion) were framing how each party was approaching the matters being debated.

A year earlier, the philosopher Christoph Hoerl had given a Lent address in the same space on the nature of time, during which told this story:

> In March 1955, after receiving news of the death of his old friend and fellow physicist Michele Besso, Albert Einstein writes the following in a letter of condolence to Besso's family: 'Now he has departed from this strange world a little ahead of me. That means nothing. People like us, who believe in physics, know that the distinction between past, present and future is only a stubbornly persistent illusion.' In retrospect, these lines are lent an added poignancy by the fact that Einstein's own death was just around the corner when he wrote them. He died just one month and three days later, on 18th April 1955. (Hoerl, 2015)

And he concluded by saying that how we understand the nature of time has tremendous significance. Within the context of these big future questions about continuing personal existence and the nature of time come the pressing matters of what the future holds for stories of the Church and for local churches on a year-by-year basis.

Some stories about the future are perhaps too conventional to be of much interest. Many churches in the UK are currently nurturing future stories in which their buildings are going to be much more available for community use. The story is often told with the suggestion that, historically, churches belonged to the community and were used much more widely than just for religious purposes. The future story being told shows this happening again, with churches becoming multi-use buildings, which would help pay for the maintenance of the building, make the building more familiar to people who may not have set foot in it before, and serve the community of which they are part. The problem with this story is that it may have become so widespread as to be a conventional aspiration, rather than a story for a particular church. Everybody is saying this is what they want to do, including quite a lot of churches in areas where there are already plenty of buildings available for community use, so the story lacks any distinctive bite.

With future stories, we need to ask whether the church owns the story. Is the envisaged future the aspiration of one person, or a few members, or is it owned more widely? If David's recruitment story had not been told at departmental meetings, before research seminars, and over the coffee machine and the photocopier, and if it had not been developed in the light of other people's comments and retelling of the story, it could have become a dangerous fantasy. It is in the telling and retelling of the story in a community, the multi-authoring of a story by a group that then owns it, that good future stories evolve.

8 Use traditional opportunities to tell the story of what is happening

We have recently seen a comprehensive school give an object lesson in how not to tell the story of what is going on. The local newspaper had a report, taken from the school's website, which said that the head teacher had been 'placed on special leave'. No explanation was offered, but it was said in the report that he had, the previous week, announced that there were to be 15 redundancies among the staff. The following week, the local paper had no more information, but gave a little more explanation for the redundancies, which they attributed to a falling roll of pupils as other schools in the area had become more popular. The chair of governors, to whom the head teacher reports, was asked about what was going on, and his reply was 'no comment'. In the absence, over several weeks, of any more detail from the school, stories about what had happened to cause the sudden departure of the head teacher started circulating in the town. We have no means of knowing whether these stories were true, and nor did the thousands of parents, prospective parents, pupils, and staff of the school, nor the rest of the population of the town and the surrounding area. But the fact that the school did not engage in telling its story (which, for all we know, may have been the result of legal advice) does not mean that a story did not get told. If possible, the school would have done much better to use the opportunities it was given to tell its story. Churches are often wary of the press and local broadcasting media through fear of being misrepresented. In one sense they are right; they will not feel that the published or broadcast material gets it exactly right, but that is not usually intentional, merely the result of busy people, for whom this is one of many stories, doing their best in the time they have got. If we are misrepresented, that is a learning opportunity for us to tell the story better next time.

Local print and broadcast media are perpetually short of material and, contrary to what some churches fear, they are not out to get you. They want to tell your story in such a way that the church members will go on buying their paper or listening to their programme. They are often an open door for churches to tell their stories. David's business school scored highly in national press and broadcast media by organizing itself so that it could offer an expert to comment, write an article, or give a television interview quickly on a wide range of topics when they came up; these were free opportunities to tell the story of the school. One minister we knew cultivated his relationship with the reporter covering the part of the city where his church was. He could head off misleading stories very quickly with a phone call.

Many other traditional local channels are available for story-telling in the church. There are pew sheets, the church magazine, the church council, the annual general meeting, the social events, the post-church coffee. Different channels will work well as story-telling places in different churches. In the churches that he has served, Vaughan has always contributed to the magazine but never acted as editor, whereas he has always edited the weekly newsletter (and in two churches started one) because he believes this is one of the most important means of sharing ongoing stories from those communities. Companies sometimes refer to 'the water cooler', the place where people most naturally gather to tell and hear stories about what is going on. The issue is to find your water cooler, or more historically your parish pump, the place where people naturally expect to tell and to hear stories. In some companies this happens where the smokers gather outside the building, and it could be important to be networked into that group even if you do not smoke and have no excuse for attending! We think it is very important for all those involved in leading in churches to find their parish pump, their water cooler, and to be in touch with the stories being told there.

9 Use every social media opportunity to tell the story of what is happening

Although there are honourable exceptions, many of those involved in church leadership are not 'digital natives'. They were born and formed before the current range of social media became available. They sometimes feel left behind; if they talk about Facebook, they find the younger people in the church have moved on to other apps. Social media emphasize more than other forms of storytelling why we need many people involved in the telling and retelling of stories. Telling stories on social media is likely to come more naturally to younger people, although it is enthusiastically practised by many older people, as demonstrated by Donald Trump's notorious Twitter habit.

Social media have recently had a bad press because it is easy to spread 'fake news'. Many people use news apps that find stories for them, that support their own view of the world – the echo-chamber effect which we talked about in Chapter 4. It appears, however, that this is only a surprise to older people, and that younger users already knew this. No longer are there journalists and editors basing their careers on the quality of the accounts they give. However, this is no reason for churches not to make the most use of social media. For example, when you move house and are looking for a church in your area, you no longer go round reading notice boards. Now you do your search online, with the church website fulfilling the role that the notice board used to have. Facebook pages are often a good way of keeping the storytelling going in a church, and the number of church leaders using Twitter seems to grow all the time. Some of those who do not like this ask what you can really say in 140 characters but, as any tweeter could tell them, this misses the point. Social media have the great strength of pointing the reader to other social media, so you can follow up the tweets that interest you by following their references to the blogs, websites etc. that give you more detail. Vaughan has adopted a similar approach to storytelling on social media as to traditional media in the present church that he serves. The website and Facebook page are edited by others while he is responsible for the Twitter feed.

A theme throughout this book has been that, where storytelling is lively and healthy, it is also difficult to control. Understanding organizations in general and churches in particular as storytelling arenas must also recognize that this puts them beyond the control of one individual or one group. People tell stories in their own way, with their own embellishments, emphasizing their own preoccupations. Inviting other members of your church to get involved in the storytelling via social media is likely to involve more people in the storytelling of the church, to bring in more voices, and thus to broaden the life of the church. So get others to do it!

10 Encourage others to share in the narrative

Leading by story does not necessarily mean being the storyteller. It means recognizing the importance of stories to the life and development of the church, valuing the storied nature of what is going on, and encouraging growth in the narrative garden or curating stories in the narrative gallery. Leaders can encourage some stories to develop, can tend and water them, maybe prune and shape them, possibly dump some manure on them, perhaps weed around them and plant another story that they think is missing, but they cannot control them. The only way to be fully in control of the garden is to put it down to decking, so that there is no intrusion of life and energy. Alternatively, if you find that the curating metaphor illuminates your story better, leaders can choose some items to exhibit, give them better or worse exposure, and develop the story boards that give the gallery its coherence, but they cannot control the impact of the exhibited items on those who come to see them. The energized organization will break out in stories, with many storytellers who will tell their stories differently but will have a degree of trust in the sensemaking and sharing of others. This will not always be the case; sometimes a story needs to be countered, to be signalled as a misunderstanding, but most of the time the church that is fully alive will be full of people enjoying one another's different stories about the life they are all engaged in, even if they contest them.

Sometimes this encouragement to share in the narrative can be done quite literally. In 2016 St Mary's, Warwick organized an exhibition of two of the world's most famous collections of stories: a First Folio of William Shakespeare's plays and a first edition of the King James edition of the Bible to commemorate the four hundredth anniversary of Shakespeare's death. This was a tangible way of enabling individuals, civic groups, schools and other organizations to write some of the most well-known stories in human culture into their stories. The most visible way we encouraged this was by setting up a means for visitors to record their reactions and tell their stories in response to seeing the two manuscripts. On the one hand some expressed their gratitude to the Bard, including a former miner who recalled how he and others narrowly escaped from a pit accident and celebrated by reading an extract from *Henry V*. On the other hand, someone recalled how miserable he was when he was made to read Shakespeare at school and what a relief it was to give it up.[2]

By contrast, one of us knew an elderly couple where he was always correcting her stories. She would tell a story to friends, and he would be unhappy about the impression the story was giving, and correct the context. They survived more than 60 years of marriage, and she never seemed to mind, but it always seemed sad that he was not prepared to trust her storytelling and her perception of the situation a little more. The good news is that he was listening, otherwise he would not have been so uncomfortable about the message he thought she was conveying. The bad news is that he always wanted to remain in control of her stories. She coped with this by telling stories in her own way when he was not there. We will all have seen examples of this desire to control, or at least finesse, others' storytelling within churches. It shows a lack of trust, or alternatively a lack of appreciation of the alternative view being expressed, and it is not healthy for a good storytelling community.

We quoted the view early in this book that we are *homo narrans narrator*, that our nature is to be both storytellers and stories. If there are people in your church who are not storytellers, something is going wrong. Something is stopping them from engaging, from producing their own narrative, and their energy and contribution are not being fully released. If there are people who are not stories, or who do not seem aware of their story or of where they are within it, then they need to find people to tell their story to in order to get to hear it themselves. Given the opportunity, we all like to tell stories about anything or anyone that we care about, and we need to tell these stories to know who and where we are. How do I know what I think until I hear what I say? How do I know what I care about and what I am prepared to give energy to until I hear my story?

If the production of stories is, and should be, beyond the control of hierarchies and authorities, the same is also true about how they spread and are passed on. A good story, in the sense of one that is worth retelling and has narrative truth, gets all over the place in no time, whether it is positive or negative. We know that we listen to a story with part of our attention given to working out how we are going to retell it, how it can be built into our fund of stories. To leave the understanding of stories and how they spread to others is a dereliction of leadership.

11 The eleventh of our ten ideas for the practice of leading by story

Underlying the ten points above is one common feature, which is that leading needs to involve enabling people to tell their stories, hearing the stories that are being told, and enabling others to hear the stories too. This is not easy. Everybody is busy, and the pace of life is fast. Some of our sisters and brothers are not very good at telling their stories, and take for ever to get to the point. Sometimes you wonder if there is ever going to be a point. And all the time you spend listening is time that could have been spent on advancing the Mission Action Plan. Listening attentively enough to hear what matters to the speaker is very tiring and, worse still, having heard you may need to help the person to develop or rewrite their story, or to act on what they have told you. You may also have to recognize that some of the things you are doing, previously unbeknown to you, play out in a very unhelpful way in this other person's story.

There are times not to listen. Sometimes someone will get stuck in telling a story for no purpose that they can remember or that we can discern. It may not be helpful for us to reinforce that story for them by listening seriously and giving it a status which it does not even have for them by the time they have finished telling it. Storytelling is done in the moment, and we all have our less distinguished moments. However, the fact that we should not give all stories as much time as their tellers might like does not mean that we should not be listening better. For many, the experience of being listened to is rare, and, as we said earlier, when people know they are being listened to, they gradually repeat themselves less and hone their stories better. Active listening values the story as well as the storyteller, and is key to leading by story.

There are also different intentions that we can bring to our listening. We should be suspicious of instrumental listening, the listening that we do in order to put someone right, in order to be able to lead them more effectively. We can detect whether someone who is listening to us is doing it in the categories that Wells (2015) characterizes as 'acting for' us, where they want to hear our situation and improve it, 'acting with' us, where they want to help us organize ourselves to make things better, 'being for' us, where they want to support people like us, or 'being with' us, where the emphasis is on the encounter itself, on accepting a stillness and presence in hearing and enabling the story, and not just hearing it in order to do something. We can all tell the difference in how our stories are being heard, and Wells argues that 'being with' is more true to the spirit of Jesus than the other approaches. Can we lead by story in a more Christ-like way by 'being with' more and leading less?

Go forth and multiply the stories

There is a fund of mostly well told stories available at The Moth[3] and they usually end their weekly podcast with a kind of secular blessing: 'May you have a story-worthy week.'

Our hope for our readers is that they will live great stories, and that this book will have contributed to their understanding of themselves as stories, and liberated them in some way to live their stories more fully. We also hope that they will enable great stories, whether by telling them or nurturing others in their telling of them. We hope that both the stories our readers live and the stories they tell and nurture will lead to healthy, flourishing and lively churches, where stories blossom freely, where they are told by many people, and where they contest gently with each other, thereby producing new stories.

May you have a story-worthy experience of leading by story.

Notes

1 We are indebted to Canon Dr James Steven of Sarum College for this image.

2 The full video is still available here: www.stmaryswarwick.org.uk/index.php?/stmarys/visiting, accessed 30.3.2017.

3 www.themoth.org.

References

Alexander, Loveday and Higton, Mike. (eds.), 2016, *Faithful Improvisation? Theological reflections on church leadership*, London: Church House Publishing.

Alldrit, Nicolas, 1998, 'Cathedrals and their communities' in Stephen Platten and Christopher Lewis (eds.), *Flagships of the Spirit: Cathedrals in society*, London: Darton, Longman and Todd, pp. 35–49.

Alvesson, M. and Spicer, A., 2011, *Metaphors We Lead By: Understanding leadership in the real world*, London and New York: Routledge.

Alvesson, M. and Spicer, A., 2016, *The Stupidity Paradox: The power and pitfalls of functional stupidity at work*, London: Profile Books.

Anderson, R. C., 2010, 'Story lines for redemptive leadership' in L. A. Golemon, (ed.), *Teaching Our Story: Narrative leadership and pastoral formation*, Herndon, VA: Alban Institute, pp. 109–23.

Bakan, D., 1966, *The Duality of Human Existence: Isolation and communion in western man*, Boston, MA: Beacon Press.

Barthes, R., 1974, *S/Z: An essay*, trans. Richard Miller, New York: Hill and Wang.

Bass, D. B., 2010, 'Living the story' in L. A. Golemon (ed.), *Living Our Story: Narrative leadership and congregational culture*, Herndon, VA: Alban Institute, pp. 151–8.

Beaumont, S., 2010, 'Giants and grasshopppers: Stories that frame congregational anxiety' in L. A. Golemon (ed.), *Finding Our Story: Narrative leadership and congregational change*, Lanham, MD: Rowman and Littlefield, pp. 91–104.

Behrens, James, 1998, *Practical Church Management: A guide for every parish*, Leominster: Gracewing.

Bellah, Robert N., 2011, *Religion in Human Evolution: From the Paleolithic to the Axial age*, Cambridge, MA and London: Belknap Press.

Bennis, W. G., 1970, 'A funny thing happened on the way to the future', *American Psychologist* 25: 595.

Bennis, Warren and Nanus, Burt, 2004, *Leaders: The strategies for taking charge*, 2nd edn, New York: Harper Business.

Billings, Alan, 2010, *Making God Possible: The task of ordained ministry present and future*, London: SPCK.

Block, P., 1993, *Stewardship: Choosing service over self-interest*, San Francisco: Berrett-Koehler.

Blomberg, Craig, 2009, 'Jesus, sinners, and table fellowship', *Bulletin for Biblical Research* 19: 35–62, available at www.ibr-bbr.org/files/bbr /bbr19a03.pdf, accessed 31.3.2017.

Boje, D., 1991, 'The storytelling organization: A study of story performance in an office-supply firm', *Administrative Science Quarterly* 36: 106–26.

Boje, D., 2001, *Narrative Methods for Organizational and Communication Research*, London: Sage.

Boje, D. M., 2008, *Storytelling Organizations*, London: Sage.

Boje, D., 2012, 'Reflections: What does quantum physics of storytelling mean for change management?', *Journal of Change Management* 12(3): 253–71.

Booker, Christopher, 2004, *The Seven Basic Plots: Why we tell stories*, London and New York: Continuum.

Bosch, David J., 1991, *Transforming Mission: Paradigm shifts in theology of mission*, Maryknoll, NY: Orbis Books.

Bourgeault, C., 2004, *Centering Prayer and Inner Awakening*, Plymouth: Cowley.

Brandes, Donna and Ginnis, Paul, 1986, *A Guide to Student-Centred Learning*, Oxford: Blackwell.

Brock, Rita Nakashima and Parker, Rebecca Ann, 2008, *Saving Paradise: How Christianity traded love of this world for crucifixion and empire*, Boston, MA: Beacon Press.

Brown, A., 2014, *The Myth of the Strong Leader: Political leadership in the modern age*, London: The Bodley Head.

Brown, Andrew and Woodhead, Linda, 2016, *That Was the Church That Was: How the Church of England lost the English people*, London and New York: Bloomsbury.

Cameron, Helen, 2010, *Resourcing Mission: Practical theology for changing churches*, London: SCM Press.

Cannadine, D., 1983, 'The context, performance and meaning of ritual: The British monarchy and the "invention of tradition", c. 1820–1977' in E. J. Hobsbawm and T. O. Ranger (eds), *The Invention of Tradition*, Cambridge: Cambridge University Press, pp. 101–64.

Capps, Donald, 1990, *Reframing: A new method in pastoral care*, Minneapolis: Fortress Press.

Carroll, Jackson W., 2011, *As One with Authority: Reflective leadership in ministry*, 2nd edn, Eugene, OR: Cascade Books.

Christie, J. R. R. and Orton, F., 1988, 'Writing a text on the life', *Art History* 11(4): 543–63.

Church of England, 2014a, *From Anecdote to Evidence: Findings of the Church Growth Research Programme 2011–2013*, available at www.churchgrowthresearch.org.uk/UserFiles/File/Reports/FromAnecdote ToEvidence1.0.pdf, accessed 30.3.2017.

Church of England, 2014b, *Talent Management for Future Leaders and Leadership Development for Bishops and Deans: A New Approach: Report of the Lord Green Steering Group*, available at www.churchofengland.org/media/2130591/report.pdf, accessed 30.3.2017.

Church of England, 2015, *Senior Church leadership: A resource for reflection: Report of the Faith and Order Commission*, available at www.churchofengland.org/media/2145175/senior%20church%20 leadership%20faoc.pdf, accessed 31.3.2017.

Coakley, Sarah, 2013, *God, Sexuality, and the Self*, Cambridge: Cambridge University Press.

Cocksworth, Christopher, 2015, 'Learning the Church: Ecclesiological thought and ecclesial practice', *International Journal for the Study of the Christian Church* 15(2): 73–88.

Collins, J., 2001, *Good to Great: Why some companies make the leap and others don't*, New York: Harper Business.

Conan Doyle, A., 1893/1993, 'Silver Blaze' in *The Memoirs of Sherlock Holmes*, New York: Oxford University Press.

Conant, Douglas and Norgaard, Mette, 2011, *Touch Points: Creating powerful leadership connections in the smallest of moments*, San Francisco: Jossey-Bass.

Connor, S., 2014. 'After it was revealed that shamed "crystal Methodist" Co-op boss Paul Flowers scored top marks, we ask: Does psychometric testing actually work?' *Independent*, 31 January, available at www.independent.co.uk/news/science/after-it-was-revealed-that-shamed -crystal-methodist-co-op-boss-paul-flowers-scored-top-marks-we -ask-9100057.html, accessed 20.3.2017.

Craddock, Fred, 2001, *Craddock Stories*, ed. Mike Graves and Richard F. Ward, St Louis, MO: Chalice Press.

Croft, Steven, 2016, *The Gift of Leadership According to the Scriptures*, Norwich: Canterbury Press.

Cupitt, D., 1988, *The Sea of Faith*, Cambridge: Cambridge University Press.

Czarniawska, B., 1997, *Narrating the Organization*, Chicago, IL: University of Chicago Press.

de Mello, Anthony, 1984, *The Song of the Bird*, New York: Image Books.

de Waal, Esther, 1990, *The Rule of St Benedict*, trans. Abbot David Parry, Leominster: Gracewing.

Denning, Steve, 2001, *The Springboard: How storytelling ignites action in knowledge-era organizations*, London: Routledge.

Denning, Steve, 2008, Interview with Michael Krull on the secret language of leadership, available at www.youtube.com/watch?v=_CTp-1VpEqs, accessed 31.3.2017.

Denning, Steve, 2011a, *The Secret Language of Leadership: How leaders inspire action through narrative*, Chichester: Wiley.

Denning, Steve, 2011b, *The Leader's Guide to Storytelling: Mastering the art and discipline of business narrative*, San Francisco: Jossey-Bass.

Denzin, Norman K. (1996), 'Sociology at the end of the century', *Sociological Quarterly* 37(4): 743–52.

Drane, John, 2000, *The McDonaldization of the Church: Spirituality, creativity, and the future of the church*, London: Darton, Longman and Todd.

Dulles, Avery, 1987, *Models of the Church*, 2nd edn, New York: Doubleday Image Books.

Dyrness, William A., 2011, *Poetic Theology: God and the poetics of everyday life*, Grand Rapids, MI and Cambridge: Eerdmans.

Edwards, L., 2000, 'A narrative journey to understanding self', M.Phil. Dissertation, Brunel University, London.

Fancourt, Graeme, 2013, *Brand New Church: The Church and the postmodern condition*, London: SPCK.

Farley, Edward, 1975, *Ecclesial Man: A social phenomenon of faith and reality*, Philadelphia, PA: Fortress Press.

Fentress-Williams, J., 2010, 'The official and unofficial story: A narrative of identity and faithfulness in the Bible' in L. A. Goleman, (ed.), *Teaching Our Story: Narrative leadership and pastoral formation*, Herndon, VA: Alban Institute, pp. 29–45.

Fidgen, J., 2017, 'Nothing but the truth', available at: www.bbc.co.uk /programmes/b086nzlg, accessed 21.3.2017.

Fineman, S., Sims, D. and Gabriel, Y., 2005/2010, *Organizing and Organizations*, 3rd/4th edn, London: Sage.

Fisk, R., 2017, 'A Trump presidency could have been avoided if Clinton had only listened to American Arabs', available at www.independent .co.uk/voices/trump-clinton-michigan-american-arabs-how-presidency -could-have-been-avoided-a7534931.html, accessed 15.2.2017.

Fitzmaurice, John, 2016, *Virtue Ecclesiology: An exploration in the good Church*, Farnham and Burlington, VT: Ashgate.

Francis, L., 2014, 'Do we have the right class of bishop?' *Church Times* 7873, 7 February.

French, R. and Simpson, P., 2011, 'Downplaying leadership: Researching how leaders talk about themselves' in D. Bell (ed.), *Political Leadership*, London: Sage, available from: http://eprints.uwe.ac.uk/12889.

Freud, S., 2015, *Civilization and Its Discontents*, Peterborough: Broadview Press.

Frye, C. Northrop, 1957, *Anatomy of Criticism: Four essays*, Princeton, NJ: Princeton University Press.

Gabriel, Yiannis, 2000, *Organizational Storytelling: Facts, fictions, fantasies*, Oxford: Oxford University Press.

Gabriel, Yiannis, 2004, *Myths, Stories, and Organizations: Premodern narratives for our times*, Oxford and New York: Oxford University Press.

Gabriel, Yiannis, 2016, 'Narrative ecologies and the role of counternarratives: The case of nostalgic stories and conspiracy theories' in S. Frandsen, T. Kuhn and M. W. Lundholt (eds), *Counter-narratives and Organization*, London: Routledge, pp. 208–26.

Ganzevoort, R. Ruard, 2011, 'Narrative approaches', in Bonnie J. Miller-McLemore (ed.), *The Wiley Blackwell Guide to Practical Theology*, Chichester and Malden, MA: Wiley, pp. 214–23.

Gharibyan-Kefalloniti, N. and Sims, D., 2012, 'Relational aesthetics and emotional relations: Leadership on board merchant marine ships', *Organization Management Journal* 9(3): 179–86.

Gladwell, M., 2008, *Outliers: The story of success*, London: Penguin.

Goffee, R. and Jones, G., 2006, *Why Should Anyone Be Led by You? What it takes to be an authentic leader*, Boston, MA: Harvard Business School Press.

Golemon, L. A., 2010a, 'Toward a framework for narrative leadership in ministry' in L. A. Goleman (ed.), *Teaching Our Story: Narrative leadership and pastoral formation*, Herndon VA: Alban Institute, pp. 1–28.

Golemon, L. A. (ed.), 2010b, *Finding Our Story: Narrative leadership and congregational change*, Herndon, VA: Alban Institute, 2010.

Golemon, L. A. (ed.), 2010c, *Living Our Story: Narrative leadership and congregational culture*, Herndon, VA: Alban Institute.

Golemon, L. A. (ed.), 2010d, *Teaching Our Story: Narrative leadership and pastoral formation*, Herndon, VA: Alban Institute.

Greenleaf, R., 1977, *Servant Leadership: A journey into the nature of legitimate power and greatness*, Mahwah, NJ: Paulist Press International.

Gregory, Brad S., 2012, *The Unintended Reformation: How a religious revolution secularized society*, Cambridge, MA and London: Belknap Press.

Grint, K., 2000, *The Arts of Leadership*, Oxford: Oxford University Press.

Grisham, T., 2006, 'Metaphor, poetry, storytelling and cross-cultural leadership', *Management Decision* 44: 486–503.

Gustafsson, C. and Lindahl, M., 2015, 'Improvisation – an emergence theory perspective', *Culture and Organization* 23(3): 1–20.

Hardy, B., 1968, 'Towards a poetics of fiction: An approach through narrative', *Novel* 2: 5–14.

Harle, T., 2012, 'The formless void as organizational template', *Journal of Management, Spirituality and Religion* 9: 103–21.

Harle, T., 2016, 'Creating Meaning Together' in Loveday Alexander and Mike Higton (eds), *Faithful Improvisation: Theological reflections on church leadership*, London: Church House Publishing, pp. 203–15.

Hauerwas, S. and Willimon, W. H., 1989, *Resident Aliens: Life in the Christian colony*, Nashville, TN: Abingdon Press.

Heaney, Maeve Louise, 2012, *Music as Theology: What music says about the Word*, Eugene, OR: Pickwick.

Hendrix, Scott H., 2015, *Martin Luther: Visionary reformer*, New Haven, CT and London: Yale University Press.

Heriot, P., 2016, *Warfare and Waves: Calvinists and charismatics in the Church of England*, Eugene, OR: Pickwick.

Hoerl, Christoph, 2015, 'Time: Experience and reality', a Lent Address at St Mary's, Warwick, available at www.stmaryswarwick.org.uk/images /uploads/Lent_2016_Christoph_Hoerl.pdf, accessed 20.3.2017.

Hopewell, James F. 1987, *Congregation: Stories and structures*, Philadelphia, PA: Fortress Press and London: SCM Press.

Hughes, Graham, 2003, *Worship as Meaning: A liturgical theology for late modernity*, Cambridge and New York: Cambridge University Press.

Humphreys, M., Ucbasaran, D. and Lockett, A., 2011, 'Sensemaking and sensegiving: Stories of jazz leadership', *Human Relations* 65: 41–62.

Hurst, David K., 2012, *The New Ecology of Leadership: Business mastery in a chaotic world*, New York: Columbia University Press.

Hybels, B., 2002, *Courageous Leadership*, Grand Rapids, MI: Zondervan.

Ibarra, Herminia, 2015, *Act Like a Leader, Think Like a Leader*, Boston, MA: Harvard Business Review Press.

Isaacs, W., 1999, *Dialogue and the Art of Thinking Together*, New York: Doubleday.

Jeffery, Paul 2004, *The Collegiate Churches of England and Wales*, London: Robert Hale.

Johansen, B., 2009, *Leaders Make the Future: Ten new leadership skills for an uncertain world*, San Francisco: Berret-Koehler.

Johnson, Mark, 1987, *The Body in the Mind: The bodily basis of meaning, imagination, and reason*, Chicago and London: University of Chicago Press.

Johnston, C., 2010, 'Story sharing and the practice of hospitality as ingredients in effective leadership' in L. A. Golemon (ed.), *Living Our Story: Narrative leadership and congregational culture*, Herndon, VA: Alban Institute, pp. 111–28.

Jones, I., 2016, *Servant Leadership: Kingdom and work bulletin no. 9*, available at www.saltleytrust.org.uk/servant-leadership-kingdom-and -work-bulletin-no-9-just-published/, accessed 18.3.2017.

Keel, T., 2007, *Intuitive Leadership: Embracing a paradigm of narrative, metaphor and chaos*, Grand Rapids, MI: Baker Books.

Kellerman, B., 2004, *Bad Leadership: What it is, how it happens, why it matters*, Cambridge MA: Harvard Business School Press.

Kellerman, B., 2008, *Followership: How followers are creating change and changing leaders*, Boston, MA: Harvard Business Review Press.

Kostera, Monika, 2012, *Organizations and Archetypes*, Cheltenham and Northampton, MA: Edward Elgar.

Küng, Hans, 1995, *Christianity: Its essence and history*, London: SCM Press.

Kupfer, Marcia (ed.), 2008, *The Passion Story: From visual representation to social drama*, Pennsylvania: Pennsylvania State University Press.

Ladkin, D., 2008, 'Leading beautifully: How mastery, congruence and purpose create the aesthetic of embodied leadership practice', *Leadership Quarterly* 19: 31–41.

Ladkin, Donna, 2010, *Rethinking Leadership: A new look at old leadership questions*, Cheltenham and Northampton, MA: Edward Elgar.

Ladkin, D. and Spiller, C. (eds.), 2013, *Authentic Leadership: Clashes, convergences and coalescences*, Cheltenham: Edward Elgar.

Lakoff, George, 1987, *Women, Fire, and Dangerous Things: What categories reveal about the mind*, Chicago: University of Chicago Press.

Lakoff, George and Johnson, Mark, 1980, *Metaphors We Live By*, Chicago: University of Chicago Press.

Lamdin, K., 2012, *Finding Your Leadership Style: A guide for ministers*, London: SPCK.

Lash, Nicholas, 1979, *Theology on Dover Beach*, London: Darton, Longman and Todd.

Laub, J., 2000, 'Assessing the servant organization: development of the organizational leadership assessment', Doctoral dissertation, Florida Atlantic University.

Linde, C., 1993, *Life Stories: The creation of coherence*, Oxford: Oxford University Press.

Lipman-Blumen, J., 2004, *The Allure of Toxic Leaders: Why we follow destructive bosses and corrupt politicians – and how we can survive them*, New York: Oxford University Press.

Loughlin, Gerard, 1996, *Telling God's Story: Bible, Church and narrative theology*, Cambridge and New York: Cambridge University Press.

MacCulloch, Diarmaid, 2009, *A History of Christianity: The first three thousand years*, London and New York: Allen Lane.

MacCulloch, Diarmaid, 2013, *Silence: A Christian history*, London and New York: Allen Lane.

MacIntyre, A., 1981, *After Virtue: A study in moral theory*, Notre Dame, IN: University of Notre Dame Press.

McKee, R., 1999, *Story: Substance, structure, style, and the principles of screenwriting*, London: Methuen.

Mandelbrot, B., 1982, *The Fractal Geometry of Nature*, San Francisco: Freeman.

Mangham, Iain L. and Overington, Michael A., 1987, *Organizations as Theatre: A social psychology of dramatic appearances*, Chichester and New York: Wiley.

Marsh, Clive, 2006, *Christ in Practice: A Christology of everyday life*, London: Darton, Longman and Todd.

Mather, M., 2010, 'Have conversations and have faith: Trading "us and them" for "all of us"' in L. A. Golemon (ed.), *Living Our Story: Narrative leadership and congregational culture*, Herndon, VA: Alban Institute, pp. 129–40.

Mead, Geoff, 2014, *Telling the Story: The heart and soul of successful leadership*, San Francisco and Chichester: Jossey-Bass.

Mead, G., 2017, 'Narrative leadership', available at https://narrativelead ershiplimited.wordpress.com/2017/02/02/podcast-narrative-leadership/, accessed 6.2.2017.

Mintzberg, Henry, Ahlstrand, Bruce and Lampel, Joseph, 1998, *Strategy Safari: The complete guide through the wilds of strategic management*, London and New York: Financial Times/Prentice Hall.

Morgan, David, 2005, *The Sacred Gaze: Religious visual culture in theory and practice*, Berkeley, CA: University of California Press.

Morgan, Gareth, 1997, *Images of Organization*, 2nd edn, Thousand Oaks, CA and London: Sage.

Morisy, Ann, 2004, *Journeying Out: A new approach to Christian mission*, London and New York: Continuum.

Moschella, M. C., 2010, 'Enlivening local stories through pastoral ethnography' in L. A. Goleman (ed.), *Teaching Our Story: Narrative leadership and pastoral formation*, Herndon, VA: Alban Institute, pp. 67–86.

NeoEnglish (2010), Northrop Frye's theory of archetypes, available at https://neoenglish.wordpress.com/2010/12/01/northrop-frye%E2%80%99s-theory-of-archetypes/, accessed 8.2.2017.

Nyhan, B. and Reifler, J., 2010, 'When corrections fail: The persistence of political misperceptions', *Political Behavior* 32: 303–30.

O'Connor, F., 1969, *Mystery and Manners: Occasional prose*, London: Macmillan.

O'Crualaoich, G., 2002, *Vernacular Narrative Tradition as Resource for Conflict/Trauma Resolution: The case of the Irish 'Wise Woman' legend*, Organizational Storytelling Seminar 3, University College Cork, Ireland.

Parker, Martin, 2002, *Against Management: Organization in an age of managerialism*, Cambridge: Polity.

Parry, K., 2008, 'Viewing the leadership narrative through alternate lenses: An autoethnographic investigation', *Management Revue* 19: 126–47.

Parry, K. and Hansen, H., 2007, 'The organizational story as leadership', *Leadership* 3: 281–300.

Peers, L., 2010, 'Expeditions into what is possible: Narrative leadership and deep change' in L. A. Golemon (ed.), *Finding Our Story: Narrative leadership and congregational change*, Lanham, MD: Rowman and Littlefield, pp. 41–58.

Percy, Martyn, 2013, 'It's not an organization: It's the Body of Christ', *Church Times*, 22 November, pp. 14 and 16.

Percy, Martyn, 2014, 'Are these the leaders we want?', *Church Times*, 12 December 2014, available at www.churchtimes.co.uk/articles/2014/12 -december/comment/opinion/are-these-the-leaders-that-we-really-want, accessed 31.3.2017.

Peters, T. J. and Waterman, R. H., 1982, *In Search of Excellence: Lessons from America's best-run companies*, New York: Warner.

Platten, Stephen and Lewis, Christopher, 2006, *Dreaming Spires? Cathedrals in a new age*, London: SPCK.

Polkinghorne, D. E., 2007, 'Validity issues in narrative research', *Qualitative Inquiry* 13: 471–86.

Pritchard, John, 2001, *Living the Gospel Stories Today*, London: SPCK.

Raelin, J., 2003, *Creating Leaderful Organizations: How to bring out leadership in everyone*, San Francisco: Berret-Koehler.

Ramsey, G. L., 2010, 'The continuous thread of revelation: Pastoral memoirs and the narrative imagination' in L. A. Golemon (ed.), *Living Our Story: Narrative leadership and congregational culture*, Herndon, VA: Alban Institute, pp. 43–62.

Rendle, G., 2010, 'Narrative leadership and renewed congregational identity' in L. A. Golemon (ed.), *Finding Our Story: Narrative leadership and congregational change*, Lanham, MD: Rowman and Littlefield, pp. 21–39.

Ritzer, George, 1993, *The McDonaldization of Society: An investigation into the changing nature of contemporary social life*, Thousand Oaks, CA: Pine Forge Press.

Roberts, Vaughan S., 1997, 'The sea of faith: After Dover Beach?', *Modern Believing* 38(3): 25–34.

Roberts, Vaughan S., 2000, 'A body of consensus? The Church as an embodied organization' in G. R. Evans and M. Percy (eds), *Managing the Church? Order and organization in a secular age*, Sheffield: Sheffield Academic Press, pp. 153–73.

Roberts, Vaughan S., 2002a, 'The Old Yew Tree', *Together for Children* 462: 23.

Roberts, Vaughan S., 2002b, 'Water as an implicit metaphor for organizational change within the Church', *Implicit Religion* 5(1): 29–40.

Roberts, Vaughan S., 2008, 'Riding waves of liturgical change' in J. Nelson (ed.), *How to Become a Creative Church Leader*, London: Canterbury Press, pp. 53–67.

Roberts, Vaughan S., 2014, 'Aquifer analysis: Told and untold stories in Warwick churches' in M. Izak, L. Hitchin and D. Anderson (eds), *Untold Stories in Organizations*, New York and London: Routledge, pp. 169–89.

Roberts, Vaughan S., 2015, 'The angel and the weeper', available at www .stmaryswarwick.org.uk/images/uploads/2015_story_AngelAndWeeper .pdf, accessed 31.3.2017.

Roberts, Vaughan S., 2017, *The Power of Story to Change a Church: Shaping the narrative of churches and communities*, Cambridge: Grove Books.

Roozen, D. A., McKinney, W. and Carroll, J. W., 1984, *Varieties of Religious Presence: Mission in public life*, Cleveland, OH: Pilgrim Press.

Runciman, D. (2013), 'Have you got "dictator envy"?', *The Week*, 30 November: 56–7.

Sadgrove, Michael, 2008, *Wisdom and Ministry: The call to leadership*, London: SPCK.

Saliers, Don E., 2007, *Music and Theology*, Nashville, TN: Abingdon Press.

Schwarz, Christian A., 2015, *The All By Itself Anglican: An introduction to Natural Church Development*, NCD Media.

Scott, S., 2009, *Fierce Leadership: A bold alternative to the worst 'best practices' of business today*, New York: Broadway Business.

Senge, P., Scharmer, C. O., Jaworski, J. and Flowers, B. S., 2005, *Presence: Exploring profound change in people, organizations and society*, London: Nicholas Brealey.

Shapiro, T., 2010, 'The sacred value of congregational stories' in L. A. Golemon (ed.), *Living Our Story: Narrative leadership and congregational culture*, Herndon, VA: Alban Institute, pp. 89–109.

Sims, D., 2003, 'Between the millstones: A narrative account of the vulnerability of middle managers' storying', *Human Relations* 56: 1195–211.

Sims, D., 2004, 'The velveteen rabbit and passionate feelings for organizations' in Y. Gabriel (ed.), *Myths, Stories and Organizations: Premodern narratives for our times*, Oxford: Oxford University Press, pp. 209–22.

Sims, D., 2005, 'Living a story and storying a life: A narrative understanding of the distributed self' in A. Pullen and S. Linstead (eds), *Organization and Identity*, London: Routledge, pp. 86–104.

Sims, D., 2010, 'Looking for the key to leadership under the lamp post', *European Management Journal* 28: 253–59.

Sims, D., 2015, 'Storying as the meaning, and the evasion of life: Reflections on when stories might be better left untold' in Michal Izak, Linda Hitchin and David Anderson (eds), *Untold Stories in Organizations*, Abingdon and New York: Routledge, pp. 13–23.

Smith, James K. A., 2009, *Desiring the Kingdom: Worship, worldview and cultural formation*, Grand Rapids: Baker Academic.

Smith, James K. A., 2013, *Imagining the Kingdom: How worship works*, Grand Rapids: Baker Academic.

Standish, N. G., 2007, *Humble Leadership: Being radically open to God's guidance and grace*, Herndon, VA: Alban Institute.

Standish, N. G., 2010, 'Pastor as narrative leader' in L. A. Golemon (ed.), *Living Our Story: Narrative leadership and congregational culture*, Herndon, VA: Alban Institute, pp. 63–88.

Steyaert, C. and Van Looy, B. (eds), 2010, *Relational Practices, Participative Organizing*, Bingley: Emerald.

Sull, D., 2010, quoted at http://missionlive.blogspot.co.uk/2010/06/biased.html, accessed 18.3.2017.

Taylor, F., 1911, *The Principles of Scientific Management*, New York: Dover.

Torry, Malcolm, 2005, *Managing God's Business: Religious and faith-based organizations and their management*, Aldershot and Burlington, VT: Ashgate.

Tourish, Dennis, 2013, *The Dark Side of Transformational Leadership: A critical perspective*, Hove: Routledge.

Walker, Keith, 1998, 'Jewels in the dust: Art in cathedrals' in Stephen Platten and Christopher Lewis (eds.), *Flagships of the Spirit: Cathedrals in society*, London: Darton, Longman and Todd, pp. 105–22.

Walker, Simon P., 2011, *The Undefended Leader Trilogy: An odyssey across the frontiers of leadership*, Human Ecology Partners.

Warren, R., 1995, *The Purpose Driven Church: Growth without compromising your message and mission*, Grand Rapids, MI: Zondervan.

Weick, K., 1995, *Sensemaking in Organizations*, London: Sage.

Weick, K., 2001, *Making Sense of the Organization*, Oxford and Malden, MA: Blackwell.

Wells, S., 2015, *A Nazareth Manifesto: Being with God*, Chichester: Wiley.

Wenger, Etienne, 1998, *Communities of Practice: Learning, meaning, and identity*, Cambridge: Cambridge University Press.

Wheatley, M., 2006, *Leadership and the New Science*, San Francisco: Berrett-Koehler.

White, William R., 1986, *Stories for Telling: A treasury for Christian storytellers*, Minneapolis, MN: Augsberg.

Williams, Margery, 1970 (first published 1922), *The Velveteen Rabbit Or How Toys Become Real*, London: William Heinemann.

Williams, R., 2003, Archbishop's Presidential Address – General Synod, York, July 2003, available at http://rowanwilliams.archbishopofcanterbury.org/articles.php/1826/archbishops-presidential-address-general-synod-york-july-2003, accessed 25.2.2014.

Woodhead, L., 2013. '"Nominals" are the Church's hidden strength', *Church Times*, 26 April, available at https://www.churchtimes.co.uk /articles/2013/26-april/comment/opinion/%E2%80%98nominals %E2%80%99-are-the-church%E2%80%99s-hidden-strength, accessed 31.3.2017.

Wright, N. T., 1992, *The New Testament and the People of God*, London: SPCK.

Index of Names and Subjects

INDEX OF NAMES AND SUBJECTS